People to Know

Georgia O'Keeffe

Legendary American Painter

Jodie A. Shull

Enslow Publishers, Inc.

40 Industrial Road   PO Box 38
Box 398   Aldershot
Berkeley Heights, NJ 07922 Hants GU12 6BP
USA   UK

http://www.enslow.com

*To my father, William Laney, our
family's artistic pioneer*

Library of Congress Cataloging-in-Publication Data

Shull, Jodie A.
    Georgia O'Keeffe: legendary American painter / Jodie A. Shull.
       v. cm. — (People to know)
    Includes bibliographical references and index.
    Contents: The search for ghost ranch—Sun prairie days—An artist's education—
Teaching art—Stieglitz and New York—Flowers larger than life—New Mexico—Desert
bones—Ladder to the sky—A change of life—Ageless beauty—Georgia O'Keeffe's legacy.
    ISBN 0-7660-2104-1 (hardcover)
      1. O'Keeffe, Georgia, 1887–1986—Juvenile literature. 2. Painters—United States—
Biography—Juvenile literature. [1. O'Keeffe, Georgia, 1887–1986. 2. Painters.
3. Women—Biography.] I. O'Keeffe, Georgia, 1887–1986. II. Title. III. Series.
    ND237.O5S58 2003
    759.13—dc21
                                2002154654

Printed in the United States of America

10 9 8 7 6 5 4 3 2 1

To Our Readers:
We have done our best to make sure all Internet Addresses in this book were active and
appropriate when we went to press. However, the author and the publisher have no con-
trol over and assume no liability for the material available on those Internet sites or on
other Web sites they may link to. Any comments or suggestions can be sent by e-mail
to comments@enslow.com or to the address on the back cover.

Every effort has been made to locate all copyright holders of material used in this book.
If any errors or omissions have occurred, corrections will be made in future editions of
this book.

Illustration Credits: *American Artists in Photographic Portraits*, Dover
Publications, Inc., 1995, p. 24; AP/Wide World Photos, pp. 45, 67, 72, 89; Photo
courtesy of Chatham Hall, formerly Chatham Episcopal Institute, p. 20;
Collection Frederick R. Weisman Art Museum at the University of Minnesota,
Minneapolis. Museum Purchase, p. 53; Gift of Georgia O'Keeffe, 1947.712,
reproduction, The Art Institute of Chicago, p. 64; Gift of Leigh B. Block,
1985.206, reproduction, The Art Institute of Chicago, p. 50; Library of
Congress, p. 38; National Archives and Records Administration, p. 60; *New
York Then and Now*, Dover Publications, Inc., 1976, p. 32; Panhandle-Plains
Historical Museum, p. 28; Photo Archives/Getty Images, p. 58; Photo courtesy
of Derrick Hasterok, p. 75; Photo by Suzanne Weinberg, p. 42; Sun Prairie
Historical Museum, p. 12; © Todd Webb, Courtesy of Evans Gallery and Todd
Webb Trust, Portland Maine USA, pp. 7, 9, 79, 83, 92, 96.

Cover Illustrations: (clockwise from top) Collection Frederick R. Weisman
Art Museum at the University of Minnesota, Minneapolis. Museum Purchase;
AP/Wide World Photos; © Corel Corporation.

Contents

Acknowledgments

To all who helped with this project, heartfelt thanks!

William Laney

Marc and Russell Whitney

The staff of the Carlsbad City Library,
Carlsbad, California

And Donna, Karen, Edith, Judith, Stephanie,
Connie, Nina, Marie, and Suzan, my host of angels

The Search for Ghost Ranch

"This is my world, but how to get into it?"[1]

O n a warm summer day in 1934, Georgia O'Keeffe bounced and swayed in her Model A Ford down a rocky dirt road. Driving was slow and sometimes dangerous in northern New Mexico. The wild empty country stretched for hundreds of miles. Forty-six-year-old O'Keeffe had learned to drive only a few years before. She was a new driver but a very determined one.

On this day, O'Keeffe was looking for the hidden road that led to a place she had heard of with the mysterious name Ghost Ranch. People told her the land around the ranch was like nothing she had ever seen before. They called it "the most beautiful place in the world."[2] This summer she especially needed to find a new and beautiful place.

Times were bad for Americans in 1934. The Great Depression had brought nationwide business failures and unemployment. Times were bad for Georgia O'Keeffe, too. America's most famous woman artist had suffered a long illness and lost her enthusiasm for painting. She had slowly begun to paint again the previous October in New York.

When summer arrived, O'Keeffe decided to leave the East and return to New Mexico. This high desert wilderness had given new life to her art before. If the stories of Ghost Ranch were true, it was a place of special beauty. The fact that it was mysterious and remote made it all the more interesting to O'Keeffe. But where was the ranch, and how did a person get there?

O'Keeffe had been looking for clues. Finally, while shopping one day in a little country store, she met a cowboy who worked at Ghost Ranch. He told her how to recognize the road that led to the cluster of ranch buildings. First, she had to cross the high wooden bridge over the Rio Grande Canyon, and then wind along the Chama River on a narrow dirt road full of gullies from heavy rain. Down a steep hillside and across a grassy plain, she saw the sign for Ghost Ranch—an animal skull resting against a rock. She was lucky. The cowboy had told her that the skulls used for road markers often got stolen.

She drove on over a bridge made of logs and found herself in a valley surrounded by high, rounded cliffs in startling colors. Layers of red, gray, green, yellow, and purple rock rose to the top of the smooth cliffs. The cabins of Ghost Ranch appeared before her in the shadow of these towering rock walls. O'Keeffe knew as

O'Keeffe found endless beauty and inspiration for her paintings in the New Mexico landscape.

soon as she saw the Ghost Ranch landscape that this was where she wanted to live and paint.[3]

Fortunately for her, the beautiful Ghost Ranch was open to visitors. She learned that her mystery place was an expensive dude ranch, where wealthy families could stay in little cottages, take hikes, and ride horses. The main ranch building, Ghost House, had a room available for the following night.

Ghost House got its name from a legend about a murder in the Spanish family that once lived there. From time to time, according to the story, a ghostly mother carrying a child came back to visit her old home.[4] For O'Keeffe, Ghost Ranch was a perfect place to work.

O'Keeffe drove the forty miles back to her rented cabin in the town of Alcalde and packed her bags. The next day she returned to Ghost Ranch and moved in for the entire summer. Unlike the other guests at the ranch, O'Keeffe was not on vacation. She spent her days alone, walking over the rocky landscape, studying the shapes of the hills, observing the colors, and absorbing everything she saw. She was at work getting ideas. Soon, what she saw began to appear in new paintings.

The rugged cliffs that O'Keeffe admired around Ghost Ranch got their color and unusual shape from ancient rocks carved by wind and water. Rock formations between one and two hundred million years old surrounded the ranch—gray shale, green and purple mudstone, pink sandstone, red and green siltstone.[5] Dinosaur bones lay buried in the hills. A prehistoric ocean and volcanoes had shaped the land, too.

From the ranch buildings, O'Keeffe could see

From the minute she saw it, Ghost Ranch captured O'Keeffe's heart.

distant mesas and mountains. Above her stretched the bright blue New Mexico sky. The colors of the land and sky were brighter and clearer in the desert than in the East, where she had lived for many years. Because of the high altitude, the air held less moisture. In the dry air, the faraway mountains looked closer and sharper. O'Keeffe made herself a bed outside to see the night sky fill with stars. She watched sunrises and sunsets bring changing color and light.

Once she found it, Georgia O'Keeffe lived at Ghost

Ranch every summer for almost fifty years. In 1940, she was able to buy a small house on the property. She painted pictures of the colorful hills again and again. As she wrote to her sister, "The country here is really fantastically beautiful. . . . I never get over being surprised that I am here . . . and that I can stay."[6]

With a place in New Mexico to come home to, O'Keeffe began a new era in her artistic career. In 1949, she left the New York art world behind to live permanently in the wide empty land of peace and quiet. Always a solitary worker, she found what she needed for her painting life in the high desert. People came to identify the Southwest region with her art and called her New Mexican home "O'Keeffe Country."

Georgia O'Keeffe is recognized today as one of the most important artists of the twentieth century. She painted for more than sixty years and produced more than two thousand works of art. New generations of Americans continue to discover and enjoy O'Keeffe's work. Her paintings of giant flowers, desert hills, and sun-bleached animal bones appear in art museums across the country.

When O'Keeffe discovered her home in the desert, she found a place that gave her joy and contentment. The road to Ghost Ranch brought her into a new world of endless artistic possibilities. "Sometimes I think I'm half-mad with love for this place," she said. "I simply cannot get enough of it."[7] O'Keeffe felt at home in the vast landscape of America's heartland. In coming to New Mexico, she was returning to open spaces like the ones of her childhood.

Sun Prairie Days

"My memories of childhood are quite pleasant."[1]

Georgia Totto O'Keeffe was born on November 15, 1887, on a prosperous dairy farm outside Sun Prairie, Wisconsin. Her parents, Francis O'Keeffe and Ida Totto O'Keeffe, had grown up on neighboring farms started by their parents. The O'Keeffes had emigrated from Ireland, and Ida's family was Dutch and Hungarian. Georgia was her parents' second child. She had a brother, Francis, who was two years older.

The vast rolling plains of southern Wisconsin were dotted with family farms in 1887. When Georgia arrived in the late autumn, the growing season had ended, and the long, harsh prairie winter was about to begin. The dark winters of extreme cold and howling wind lasted almost half the year. Georgia's first

Georgia was born on this dairy farm near Sun Prairie, Wisconsin.

months of life were spent indoors in the dim light of oil lamps and hearth fires.

The return of spring brought sunlight and warmth to the countryside. "My first memory is of the brightness of light—light all around," Georgia wrote. Many years later, she said she remembered sitting on a quilt outdoors with her mother when she was only eight or nine months old. Her mother laughed at this unlikely memory. But Georgia described the scene so perfectly that her mother had to agree. Georgia could remember things in the most remarkable way.[2]

Five more children followed Georgia in the O'Keeffe family until there were seven: older brother Francis, Georgia, Ida, Anita, brother Alexius, Catherine, and Claudia. The family was not especially large in farm country. Many hands were needed to do the endless work of taking care of the land and the animals. The O'Keeffes, the other farm workers, mother Ida's aunt Jenny, and the local schoolteacher all lived together in the big white wooden house on six hundred acres.

Georgia resembled her black-haired, blue-eyed Irish father. Like him, she had strong features and a practical, independent spirit. Francis O'Keeffe was humorous and kind and taught Georgia to play the violin. When he was not working long hours managing the dairy business, Georgia walked with him on country roads around the farm.

From her mother, Georgia learned to read, play the piano, sew, cook, and give close attention and care to everything she did. Her mother placed great value on education and made sure all the children received every opportunity to discover their talents and improve their minds. She gathered them all on the living room floor on Sunday afternoons, rainy days, and evenings and read to them.

Georgia's brother Francis had weak eyesight. Ida O'Keeffe most often read the exciting adventures he loved but could not read for himself. Georgia did not mind. She never forgot those stories of action and courage. Tales of the Old West, like *The Life of Kit*

Carson, fed her imagination. She wrote later, "I think that reading was a good start to a lot of things."[3]

When she was almost five years old, Georgia began to attend the one-room schoolhouse at the edge of the farm. Both of her parents had gone to the little school. Neither the space nor the studies had changed much since they were children. Georgia walked to school every day through the family's apple orchard, watching the sky and the meadows beyond. The natural world spread out before her—the tall grasses, the oak trees, the fields of wheat, the wildflowers in spring. Her teacher noted that Georgia liked her own company best.[4] She seemed happiest in a personal and private world where she could observe and imagine.

The solitary pleasure that Georgia enjoyed most was playing outside under the apple trees with her homemade dollhouse.[5] She had a family of small china dolls with blond hair and arms that moved. She created a dollhouse for them from a pair of wooden boards notched to fit together in the shape of a cross. Standing on edge, the boards formed the walls of four rooms for her doll family to live in.

She trimmed the tall grass around the house like a lawn, sprinkled sand pathways, and placed a pan of water nearby for a pond. A shingle floated in the pond for a boat, and twigs and leaves from the apple trees made furnishings for the house. She used her good sewing skills to make clothes for her dolls. "I believe," she later wrote, "that during the years when many children draw a great deal, I was busy with the doll family and house and garden."[6]

Georgia preferred playing alone to any group

games her sisters organized. Because she was the oldest girl, she could do as she pleased. Georgia got her privacy not only at play but also at home. While the younger girls shared bedrooms, Georgia had a room of her own in an upstairs tower her father had added to the farmhouse. The room had large windows facing north and west that looked out over the trees to the fields and woods beyond.

Ida O'Keeffe wanted her daughters' education to include both art and music. She could provide the musical instruction, but she arranged to have the schoolteacher who lived with them give the girls drawing lessons in the evenings. Beginning when Georgia was eleven, the girls practiced drawing cubes and spheres; they learned perspective, shading, and detail from a popular drawing instruction book by Louis Prang.

A year later, Georgia and her sisters began traveling to Sun Prairie by wagon every Saturday afternoon to learn watercolor painting from a local art teacher. At first, Georgia chose pictures of flowers and horses to copy from the teacher's collection. She later copied a lighthouse from her geography book and added the ocean, the sun, and some palm trees as she imagined them. She had never seen a real palm tree or the ocean.

Like most young students of her time, Georgia learned to draw and paint by copying. She tried hard to make her work match what she saw—in pictures and in the real world. She had learned to create shapes like cubes and spheres from her first drawing book. Now she was learning to paint with color and struggling to capture the shades of gray and blue and green she saw in the sky and the snow and the trees.

The summer Georgia was twelve she surprised herself by announcing to her friend Lena, "I'm going to be an artist."[7] Georgia was not sure how the idea came to her so clearly. She had found a picture that fascinated her in a book of her mother's. It was a two-inch-high pen-and-ink drawing of a girl's face. "For me, it just happened to be something special—so beautiful," she later wrote. "I believe that picture started something moving in me."[8]

Independent and curious, imaginative and solitary, Georgia found that the idea of working as an artist appealed to her. Her family recognized that Georgia had artistic ability. Her mother wanted all her daughters to develop their talents, and she encouraged Georgia to work at her art. Ida expected that her oldest daughter would make a fine art teacher someday.

The idea of a woman making a living as a professional artist in America in 1900 was beyond anyone's expectations. In an era when women were not yet allowed to vote or hold public office, women with artistic interests became art teachers. Georgia was sometimes accused by her family of having crazy notions and being stubbornly independent.[9] If the other girls wore their hair up, she wore hers down. If the others wore sashes on their dresses, Georgia left her sash at home. She lived by her own notions, crazy or not. Her dream of becoming an artist would take independence and courage.

In the fall of 1901, Georgia started high school. Her parents sent her to Sacred Heart Academy, a

Catholic boarding school for girls near Madison, Wisconsin. The O'Keeffes paid twenty dollars extra for Georgia to have art lessons that year. When the art teacher criticized her first charcoal drawing, calling it too small and too dark, Georgia's feelings were hurt. She had to hold back tears.[10]

Georgia liked her drawing the way it was, but she wanted to learn and to win her teacher's approval. After that, she wrote, "I . . . always drew everything a little larger and a little lighter than I really thought it should be."[11] At the end of the year, Georgia won the school's gold medal for drawing.

The next fall, Georgia and her older brother, Francis, were sent to the big public high school in Madison. They lived with their mother's sister, Lenore "Lola" Totto, and attended school together. Georgia's art teacher that year brought a flower to class for the students to study and draw. It was a common wild-flower called jack-in-the-pulpit that Georgia had seen many times in the woods. When the teacher pointed out the remarkable shape and color of the flower, Georgia made a discovery. "She started me looking at things—looking very carefully at details."[12] Georgia had spent her childhood years enjoying the woods and fields around her home. Her memory was filled with images of the natural world, the trees, flowers, and plants. In her second year of high school, she gained the simple but powerful idea of looking at those images more closely.

An Artist's Education

"I was taught to paint like other people."[1]

While fifteen-year-old Georgia was finishing the school year in Madison, her parents made a big decision for the family. In the fall of 1902, the O'Keeffes sold their Wisconsin farm for $12,000 and moved to Williamsburg, Virginia. Georgia's father decided he must escape the bitter cold Wisconsin winters. All his brothers had died of tuberculosis, a deadly lung disease. He hoped the warmer southern climate would preserve his health.

At the close of the school year, Georgia and her brother Francis joined the family in Williamsburg in June 1903. Their father had purchased a large house and some land and a grocery store. At the end of the summer, Georgia left home once again to attend a girls boarding school in the small town of Chatham, Virginia, two hundred miles from home.

Georgia was almost sixteen when she arrived at Chatham Episcopal Institute to complete her high school education. Talking about Georgia, one of her fellow students said that "this strongminded girl knew what suited her and would not be changed."[2]

Georgia was admired for her excellent sewing ability. She had once made beautiful doll clothes. Now she made clothes for herself. She also played basketball, joined the German club, and served as treasurer of the tennis team. Her nickname was Georgie.

Georgia had lived away from her family for the past two years and had learned to take care of herself. The other students liked Georgia for her independent ways and her sense of humor and playfulness. She broke the school rules by sneaking out for long walks in the country. "Now, what can I do that I shouldn't do and not get caught?" she thought.[3]

Luckily for Georgia, the principal at Chatham was also the art teacher and understood Georgia well. Elizabeth May Willis recognized her young student's artistic ability and the personality behind it. Miss Willis forgave Georgia's rebellious behavior and allowed her to work at her own pace in the art studio. She said to the other students, "When the spirit moves Georgia, she can do more in a day than you can do in a week."[4]

Georgia was also able to continue her music education at Chatham. She took piano lessons and played in a school recital. Georgia had learned how to play the violin from her father and had always loved music as well as art. In 1922, she told a newspaper reporter, "Singing has always seemed to me the most perfect means of expression. . . . And after singing, I think the violin. Since I cannot sing, I paint."[5]

The other students recognized that Georgia had a very special talent. She was chosen as the art editor of the school's first yearbook, *Mortar Board.* Her classmates wrote about her, "O is for O'Keeffe, an artist divine; / Her paintings are perfect and her

The other girls at Chatham admired Georgia, second from right, for her independent spirit and terrific sense of humor. Here, she and her friends appear to be getting a scolding.

drawings are fine."[6] Miss Willis encouraged Georgia to concentrate on her art work. At the end of her senior year, she gave Georgia the school art prize for her painting of red-and-yellow corn.

Georgia O'Keeffe graduated from high school in June 1905 at the age of seventeen. She had always had difficulty with spelling and had to take a required spelling test many times before finally passing it. "I never did learn to spell," said Georgia.[7]

With the encouragement of her art teacher and her classmates at Chatham, Georgia believed in her artistic ambitions enough to set out for the Art Institute of Chicago in September 1905. Founded in 1879, the Art Institute was one of America's largest art museum schools. Like other art schools of the time, the Art Institute of Chicago taught students to copy the realistic style of the great painters of Europe.

Georgia O'Keeffe was one of nine hundred students enrolled at the institute that fall. By February, she was ranked first in her intermediate class. Of her year at the institute, she remembered most the lessons in drawing and composition given by John Vanderpoel. Vanderpoel was a well-known artist, born in Holland. "He was a very kind, generous little man—one of the few real teachers I have known," Georgia later wrote.[8]

At the end of the school year, Georgia returned to her family in Virginia. The O'Keeffes were finding that the warm, humid climate of Williamsburg brought health hazards, too. Tropical diseases like malaria and typhoid fever struck the family. That summer

Georgia came down with typhoid fever, a bacterial illness that could be deadly. Her fever became so high that her long straight hair fell out. By September 1906, her health was no longer in danger. As she recovered her strength, her hair slowly grew back in curls.

It was too late in the year to return to the Art Institute, so Georgia spent the 1906–1907 school year at home recovering from her illness. She lived with her parents, Aunt Jenny, and her three youngest siblings—Alexius, Catherine, and Claudia. The neighborhood children liked to play at the O'Keeffe house, where Georgia often took them for walks in the woods. "Georgia was great fun with the children—she was like her father that way," a neighbor said.[9]

In September 1907, Georgia was on her way again to study art in the city. This time she traveled to the Art Students League in New York. Her high school teacher Elizabeth Willis had studied there and encouraged Georgia to continue her art education in New York. Georgia made the twelve-hour train trip into the bustling heart of America's largest city.

Georgia O'Keeffe was almost twenty years old when she arrived in New York. She rented a room near the league for a few dollars a week. Her fellow art students later described her as a beautiful girl with "a captivating dimpled grin, expressive intelligent features, slim boyish grace."[10] Because her last name was O'Keeffe, the students gave her the Irish nickname "Patsy." Her hair was still growing out from her recent illness. Her friends liked to run their fingers through her short curls, so unusual at a time when most women had long hair.

At the league, O'Keeffe studied still life—the painting of objects—with the famous American art teacher William Merritt Chase. He gave the students the assignment of painting a new painting every day—on the same canvas. They had to paint over and over on the same surface until it could not hold any more paint. O'Keeffe learned a great deal from him about the use of painting materials. "His love of style—color—paint as paint—was lively. I loved the color in the brass and copper pots and pans, peppers, onions, and other things we painted for him."[11]

O'Keeffe was learning how to master the materials used by an artist, but she was not learning how to create art of her own imagining. Her teachers asked students to copy the style and subject matter of the great artists who had come before them—mostly Europeans. O'Keeffe became very good at copying the style of her teachers. "If you study with anyone, you try to do what they're trying to teach you," she said.[12] At the end of the school year, she won the top prize for a painting of a dead rabbit lying beside a copper pot.

One man in New York who did not agree with the practice of copying the art of the past was Alfred Stieglitz. A pioneer in the field of photography, Stieglitz ran a small art gallery in Manhattan. There he exhibited the paintings and photographs he liked, most created in new, nontraditional styles. He hoped to establish a modern, American art community that did not rely on models of the past. The winter that O'Keeffe was studying at the Art Students League, Stieglitz

The famous artist William Merritt Chase advised O'Keeffe to "be artistic in every way."

hosted a controversial exhibit of drawings by the French sculptor Auguste Rodin. The drawings were considered a shocking change from the realistic style taught at art school.

O'Keeffe went with her friends to see the Rodin drawings at Stieglitz's Little Galleries of the Photo-Secession. The galleries were in the attic of an old brownstone mansion at 291 Fifth Avenue and came to be called, simply, 291. Visitors had to ride an elevator that was raised and lowered by a rope. O'Keeffe was not very impressed by the Rodin drawings, but she remembered meeting the colorful Alfred Stieglitz, with his loud voice and strong opinions about art.

O'Keeffe returned home to Williamsburg in the summer of 1908 to find her family in serious financial trouble. Her father's efforts to start a business in Virginia had not been successful. The prosperous farming life the family had enjoyed in Wisconsin had disappeared with their move. There was not enough money for Georgia to continue art school.

At this time, Georgia O'Keeffe was forced to reconsider her ambition to be a professional artist. It was very difficult for a woman to make a living as an artist at the beginning of the twentieth century. Few women tried it. Without enough money and the guidance of an art college, how did one get started? Although she was not sure of her own direction as a painter, O'Keeffe did not like the idea of copying the successful artists of the past. "Why have as an aim the copying of paintings so great they can never be copied?" she asked.[13]

Two days before her twenty-first birthday, she left

Williamsburg to look for a job. She traveled to Chicago, where she could live with her mother's relatives while she worked. O'Keeffe had enough art training to work as an illustrator. A family friend helped her find a position drawing lace and embroidery in advertisements for ladies' dresses. She had to be very careful and very quick. That job, she later said, taught her to work hard and not waste a moment of time.[14]

Although she was good at illustration, this work had little to do with the artistic dreams that had taken O'Keeffe to art school. She was not happy working in the city at a job that did not use her creative talents.[15] After two years in Chicago, she came down with the measles, a disease that can weaken the eyes. Drawing detailed illustrations day after day was also very hard on her eyes. O'Keeffe decided to go back to Virginia.

When she returned to her family around 1910, Georgia O'Keeffe found that their situation had not improved. They had sold their large Williamsburg home. Her mother had come down with tuberculosis, the dreaded disease that had killed many O'Keeffe family members in the past. Seeking a drier climate that might benefit Ida O'Keeffe's health, the family moved to Charlottesville.

Charlottesville, home of the University of Virginia, was located in the gently rolling mountains of central Virginia. There the family opened a boardinghouse for students. All five O'Keeffe sisters were living at home with their parents in June 1912 when Ida and Anita returned to the University of Virginia summer school. Summer was the only session that women were permitted to attend at the university, and most were studying to be teachers.

By this time, Georgia O'Keeffe had decided to give up the idea of becoming a professional artist. Anita persuaded her to visit a drawing class at the university. The teacher was Alon Bement, a professor of fine arts from Columbia University's Teachers College in New York. Bement taught his students the principles of the famous art educator Arthur Wesley Dow, who had invented a method of teaching art as self-expression. O'Keeffe liked Dow's idea that creating art is simply "filling a space in a beautiful way."[16] The artist could decide for herself what is beautiful.

From Dow's principles, O'Keeffe learned that "art could be a thing of your own."[17] She followed Alon Bement to all of his classes that day and signed up for summer school at the university. After her years of copying models of drawing and painting, she welcomed the idea that an artist could invent a style of her own. Her work was so good that Bement invited her to return the following year to be one of his teaching assistants.

Later that summer, O'Keeffe heard from a high school friend about a job opening for a drawing teacher in Amarillo, Texas. She had no experience as a teacher and no college degree, but she received excellent recommendations from her former art professors for her job application. She was hired. In mid-August 1912, at the age of twenty-four, she boarded a westbound train for Texas.

Georgia always knew that she wanted to be an artist. She began her art career as a teacher.

4

Teaching Art

"I feel like myself—and I like it."[1]

As a child, Georgia O'Keeffe had listened eagerly to stories of the Wild West. Her mother had read aloud to Georgia and her brothers and sisters as often as she could, and the popular western adventures of the day had been their favorites. Now O'Keeffe would be traveling as far west as she had ever been. The train ride took her to Amarillo, Texas.

In 1912, Amarillo was a rough and dusty cattle-shipping town. O'Keeffe rented a room at the Magnolia Hotel. She ate her meals in the dining room, where she could observe the cowboys, gamblers, and travelers passing through town. To her, the vast, flat country around Amarillo was exciting and beautiful. She enjoyed watching the wild weather—the tornadoes, dust storms, prairie fires—and the colorful sunrises and sunsets. "That was my country," she said. "Terrible winds and a wonderful emptiness."[2]

O'Keeffe's job as supervisor of drawing and penmanship for the Amarillo school district was her first teaching experience. She discovered how much she liked teaching art. "I wondered why I should be paid for what I was doing," she said.[3] Instead of having her students copy pictures out of textbooks, she encouraged them to draw things from their everyday lives.

In the summer of 1913, O'Keeffe returned home to Charlottesville to teach summer school at the university. Her sister Catherine noticed a change in Georgia's drawing style after her first year in Texas. "Georgia seemed to be drawing just for herself, and her work was like that of no one else."[4]

While she lived in Charlottesville, O'Keeffe took long walks and went camping in the nearby mountains with her sisters and university friends. She set up an art studio in the basement of her family's house. One of the subjects she painted was the hollyhock flowers growing in the backyard.

Impressed by the quality of her work, Professor Bement encouraged her to keep painting. He urged her to go to New York to study at Columbia University Teachers College. After a second year in Amarillo and another summer in Virginia, O'Keeffe decided to take Bement's advice. She resigned from her teaching job and headed for Columbia Teachers College.

O'Keeffe arrived in New York in the fall of 1914 after having been away from the city for seven years. She found the art world in a time of exciting transition.

In the winter of 1913, an exhibit called the Armory Show had been held to introduce the American public to new works of modern art. Hundreds of European and American paintings that broke art traditions were exhibited.

At almost twenty-seven years of age, O'Keeffe was older than most of her classmates at Columbia University Teachers College. She had very little money and lived in a rented room that cost $4 a week. With only enough money to pay for one winter of study in New York, she spent most of her attention on her art classes. She got poor grades in her other training classes for teachers. A friend wrote, "She lived on very little . . . but her colors were always the brightest, her palette the cleanest, her brushes and paints the best."[5] Professor Arthur Wesley Dow said of her, "She is one of the most talented people in art that we have ever had."[6]

While she was studying at Teachers College, O'Keeffe met another young student, Anita Pollitzer. The two became good friends, although Pollitzer was seven years younger than O'Keeffe. Because Pollitzer was very interested in modern art, she often visited 291, the famous gallery of Alfred Stieglitz. Sometimes she took O'Keeffe along. O'Keeffe remembered Stieglitz. He was an important figure in the art world, always a promoter of the new and modern in art. He especially encouraged American artists to break away from the traditions of Europe.

Georgia O'Keeffe saw the value of visiting Stieglitz's modern art exhibits because "it showed you how you could make up your mind about what to paint."[7] The modern artists often used shapes and

New York City in the early 1900s was an exciting place for a young artist like O'Keeffe.

colors from their own imaginations. She also learned from seeing the exhibits at 291 and the sale of paintings and drawings there that artists could make a living by painting according to their own ideas.

In the summer of 1915, O'Keeffe returned to the University of Virginia to teach summer school. To stay in touch with the New York art world, she subscribed to Stieglitz's magazine *Camera Work*, which featured reproductions of modern art. She began sending her watercolors to Pollitzer for criticism.

O'Keeffe needed to go back to work. In the fall of 1915, she accepted a teaching position at Columbia College, a teachers college for women in Columbia, South Carolina. She liked the prospect of this job because it required her to teach only four classes a week. She would have plenty of free time for painting. "I had gotten a lot of new ideas and was crazy to get off in a corner and try them out," she said.[8]

O'Keeffe had time to paint and also to enjoy the natural beauty of her new home. The South Carolina autumn was warm and mild. Georgia was able to take long walks in the pine forests around the college, which was located in the foothills of the Appalachian Mountains. She wrote letters to Anita Pollitzer in New York and continued to send her the watercolors she made.

O'Keeffe spent much time thinking about her art, what she would paint and who she would paint it for. She wrote to Pollitzer that she wanted to paint something that would please Alfred Stieglitz: "I would rather have Stieglitz like something I'd done than anyone else."[9]

O'Keeffe knew she had learned well how to use an artist's materials. Now she needed to choose a subject to paint, something that would be uniquely hers. She thought about her own ideas. "I found that I could say things with color and shapes that I couldn't say in any other way," she wrote.[10]

O'Keeffe decided to start fresh and record the shapes that she could see in her head. "I have the kind of mind that transfers experience into shapes and colors," she said.[11] She put away her paints and began working in charcoal—black and white—until she could draw the shapes the way she wanted them to be. "I was alone and . . . free, working into my own, unknown—no one to satisfy but myself," she wrote.[12] The new drawings were abstract, not realistic like photographs. They were lines and shapes that expressed O'Keeffe's view of the world.

On January 1, 1916, Anita Pollitzer received a roll of drawings from Georgia O'Keeffe. When she spread them out, she saw her friend's new effort to express shapes and feelings that were in her head. "I was struck by their aliveness. They were different. . . . These drawings were saying something that had not yet been said."[13]

Pollitzer could not resist taking the remarkable drawings to Alfred Stieglitz. When he saw them, Stieglitz told Pollitzer that the drawings were the "purest, fairest, sincerest things that have entered 291 in a long while."[14] O'Keeffe wanted to know more about his reaction, and she began writing to Stieglitz herself.

Early in the spring of 1916, O'Keeffe was offered a new teaching job in Canyon, Texas. First, though, she would need to return to Columbia University Teachers College and complete Professor Dow's art methods class for teachers. O'Keeffe decided to do it. She had to leave her position in South Carolina early, after the first month of the school term, and head to New York.

One day at lunch in the cafeteria at Columbia Teachers College, O'Keeffe heard from another student that the gallery at 291 was showing the work of someone named "Virginia" O'Keeffe. Although the student had the name wrong, Georgia realized that Stieglitz must have put her charcoal drawings on exhibit. She rushed over to the gallery to investigate. O'Keeffe argued that she was not ready to put her work on public display. Stieglitz persuaded her to let him keep her pictures on the walls. "He was a good talker," O'Keeffe said later.[15]

That summer O'Keeffe visited her family home in Charlottesville for the last time. As her artistic career was coming together, her family was drifting apart. Her brothers had left home to find jobs. Her father had started a trucking business and traveled to wherever he could get work. Her sister Ida was an art teacher in another part of Virginia. Anita had married a young man from Texas. Catherine was in Wisconsin studying to be a nurse. Claudia was finishing high school. Early in May, the final blow to the family came when Georgia's mother died of tuberculosis at the age of fifty-two.

In September 1916, O'Keeffe arrived in Canyon, Texas, twenty miles south of Amarillo, to start work at a new college for training teachers. At West Texas State Normal College, in the small prairie town of

2,500 people, O'Keeffe was the only art teacher. She taught design, costuming, and interior decoration. She tried to teach her students the importance of art in everyday life. "When I taught art, I taught it as the thing everyone has to use," she said.[16] She encouraged her students to make decisions with an artistic eye, with consideration for beauty.

O'Keeffe seemed very unconventional to the people of Canyon. She was the only teacher from the East. She made her own clothes and liked simple styles in basic colors—usually black and white. She spent her Sundays taking long walks on the prairie. From the edge of Canyon, she could walk in any direction, watch the sun go down and then walk back guided by the lights of the town.

Before O'Keeffe's mother died, she had asked Georgia to look after her youngest sister, Claudia. After getting settled in Canyon, Georgia sent for Claudia and enrolled her as a student in the college for teachers. Georgia and Claudia went exploring together. They often visited Palo Duro, a deep canyon in the surface of the prairie created by the flow of a small creek. It was one thousand feet deep in some places. To get to the bottom, Georgia and Claudia had to hike down steep and slippery cattle trails.

In the scenery of Canyon, O'Keeffe found wonderful new subjects for her painting. First, she observed nature as she always did. Then she began to paint not what she saw, but what she felt about seeing it. She painted the sunrise, the sunset, the approach of a train across the prairie, and the approach of a storm. The vast flat land and the wide sky overhead, filled with clouds that moved with the constant wind, gave O'Keeffe the ideas she needed to produce many paintings that school year. She formed the habit of painting the same subject again and again until she was satisfied with the result.

During her first year in Canyon, O'Keeffe kept in touch with Stieglitz by writing letters. Stieglitz wrote to encourage her in her painting, and she sent him rolled-up drawings and paintings as she completed them. Stieglitz helped her keep up with the world of art in New York. He encouraged her to read the books of philosophy and literature that were being discussed by educated people in the city.

O'Keeffe's paintings of the land and sky around Canyon were not done in the realistic style that she had been taught at art school. Her pictures developed from the shapes and colors in her imagination and memory. Once when she showed a painting of Palo Duro to a friend, he told her, "It doesn't look like the canyon to me." She said it was a picture of her feelings about the canyon, and he said, "Well, you must have had a stomachache when you painted it!"[17] Georgia O'Keeffe was a modern artist. The residents of Canyon, Texas, were used to seeing paintings that portrayed the world with the realism of photographs.

O'Keeffe paid little attention to the friends in Canyon who laughed at her work. She had the approval of Stieglitz and the joy of creating something that was completely her own. Thinking back about her time in Texas, she later said, "It was all so far away—there was quiet and an untouched feel to the country and I could work as I pleased."[18]

"Finally, a woman on paper," said Alfred Stieglitz, who saw a woman's feelings reflected in O'Keeffe's drawings. Stieglitz went on to become one of the most important people in her life.

On April 3, 1917, Stieglitz opened Georgia O'Keeffe's first solo art show at 291 Fifth Avenue. The exhibit included her new Texas watercolors. Three days after the exhibit opened, the United States entered World War I and joined the battle against Germany that was raging in Europe. Depressed over the war and running short of money, Stieglitz wrote to O'Keeffe that he would have to close the gallery at 291 after her exhibit.

O'Keeffe wanted very much to visit New York, although she had only a little time and money. Making a quick decision, she took all her money out of the bank, packed her bag, and boarded the train heading east. Once in the city, she went to 291 to visit Stieglitz. After he had photographed her paintings on the gallery walls, he had taken them down. When O'Keeffe arrived for her surprise visit, he quickly put the paintings back up for her to see.

While she was in the city, Stieglitz introduced O'Keeffe to other talented young artists and photographers. He also took the first of his many photographs of O'Keeffe. Her brief time in New York strengthened her relationship with Stieglitz. Their friendship would change Georgia O'Keeffe's life.

5

Stieglitz and New York

"I believe that to create one's own world in any of the arts takes courage."[1]

After her visit to New York, Georgia O'Keeffe returned to Texas to spend her first summer in the Southwest. When summer school ended, Georgia and Claudia explored the Colorado Rockies. The sisters also visited northern New Mexico and spent a few days in the old capital city of Santa Fe. Located in the high desert and surrounded by mountains, Santa Fe was a popular place for artists and the home of a mixture of Hispanic and Native American people. Georgia O'Keeffe never forgot her visit. She said, "If you ever go to New Mexico, it will itch you for the rest of your life."[2]

O'Keeffe returned to her teaching job in Canyon in the fall of 1917. The depressing effects of the World War could not be ignored even in Canyon. Many of the young male students at West Texas State Normal College enlisted in the army, as did Georgia and Claudia's brother Alexius. By her thirtieth birthday in November, Georgia was having trouble doing any painting. In December, Claudia left Canyon to begin work as a student teacher in another town, leaving her sister alone.

During the cold winter of 1918, Georgia O'Keeffe could not keep warm enough. Like hundreds of thousands of Americans that year, she came down with influenza. The influenza epidemic of 1918–1919 killed 20 million people worldwide. O'Keeffe had to take a leave of absence from teaching and stay with a friend in a warm part of southern Texas to recover. When Stieglitz heard that O'Keeffe was sick and had to leave her job, he urged her to come to New York. His niece Elizabeth offered to let O'Keeffe stay at her studio apartment. O'Keeffe thought about whether she should remain in Texas or return to the city. She wanted to make the right choice, and in early June, she decided it was best for her to return to the East.

Stieglitz met O'Keeffe at the train station and took her to his niece's apartment. There she was able to rest and recover her strength. At that time, Stieglitz decided to leave his long and unhappy marriage and live with O'Keeffe. Later that summer, they visited the Stieglitz family's summer home on the shores of Lake George in the Adirondack Mountains in New York. Stieglitz and O'Keeffe had a deep admiration for each other's art. He encouraged her to paint, and her striking features inspired him to photograph her.

Georgia O'Keeffe's style of dress, mostly simple

Lake George offered O'Keeffe a new landscape for her paintings. The beautiful setting also inspired her to experiment with different painting techniques.

black clothing, and her straight black hair and bold features always attracted notice. Stieglitz also liked the color black. He often wore a long black cape over his clothing. While Stieglitz was noisy and outspoken, O'Keeffe was quiet and reserved. He loved to be in conversation with a circle of friends; she liked solitude and silence. They had become well acquainted through letters over the previous year. Although Stieglitz was fifty-four and O'Keeffe thirty, they were good friends and loving companions.

At the Lake George house, O'Keeffe had long, uninterrupted hours to explore the woods and mountains and to paint. While living in Canyon, O'Keeffe had used watercolors to capture the light, bright colors of the Texas sky and landscape. Now she began working with oil paints again. Painting with oil requires plenty of time to prepare the canvases and paints and to apply the slow-drying colors. Stieglitz encouraged her to master the oil painting techniques that were used by the male artists who exhibited at 291.

When summer came to an end, O'Keeffe had to decide whether or not to return to her teaching job in Canyon. Stieglitz asked her what she wanted more than anything else. She replied that she would like to spend a year painting full-time. Although Stieglitz had little money, he found a friend who would lend him $1,000. That was enough to give O'Keeffe a year's support so that she could leave her job and concentrate on her art. Stieglitz wanted to help her build a career as a professional artist.

O'Keeffe resigned from her teaching position in Canyon, and soon her possessions arrived from Texas in a wooden barrel. Besides her clothes and books, her old drawings and paintings were packed in the barrel. As she had done before when she wanted to make a fresh start with her work, she looked over the old pictures and decided not to keep them. She put them in a trash can to be thrown away. That night when she and Stieglitz came home, the drawings and paintings were blowing down the street in the wind.

O'Keeffe began painting full-time while she lived in the studio apartment at 114 East Fifty-ninth Street in New York City. The studio was brightly colored with yellow walls and an orange floor, filled with light from two southern windows and a skylight. Stieglitz continued his photography, and O'Keeffe experimented with her painting. "Color," she wrote, "is one of the great things in the world that makes life worth living to me."[3]

Stieglitz took many photographs of O'Keeffe. By the time he stopped using his heavy cameras when he was in his early seventies, he had made more than three hundred portraits of her. Posing for the old-fashioned camera was not easy. O'Keeffe had to remain completely still for three to four minutes for the exposures on glass plates. She laughed about the difficulty of holding still for so long. Everything began to itch just because she was not able to move.[4] Studying the photos of herself, O'Keeffe was amazed at her appearance. "I can see myself, and it has helped me to say what I want to say—in paint."[5]

Stieglitz had not been taking photographs during the years of World War I, but his relationship with O'Keeffe inspired him to work again. When his friends

Wherever she lived, O'Keeffe captured the color and beauty of her surroundings in her paintings.

saw that he was again taking pictures, they arranged for an exhibit of his work. One-third of the photographs exhibited were of O'Keeffe. In some, she was posed in front of her paintings, so viewers saw not only O'Keeffe but her work as well. The exhibit received a lot of attention in the New York art world, and O'Keeffe's name began to appear in the news.

In January 1923, O'Keeffe had a show of her own at the Anderson Galleries, a famous art auction house in New York City. One hundred of her pictures were displayed for two weeks. The flyer for the exhibit read, "Alfred Stieglitz presents one hundred pictures—Oils, water-colors, pastels, drawings by Georgia O'Keeffe, American." Stieglitz was keeping his promise to introduce O'Keeffe to the world.

The 1923 exhibit established Georgia O'Keeffe's status as a professional artist. Her experimental year as a full-time painter in New York had turned into a permanent job. People began to refer to her simply as "O'Keeffe," as Stieglitz always did. The public admired her work. She earned a remarkable $3,000 in sales of paintings from the 1923 show. Stieglitz established a tradition of annually exhibiting her work from that time on. She would paint during the summer and fall and show her new work in the early part of the following year. In March 1924, Stieglitz and O'Keeffe shared an exhibition at the Anderson Galleries—photography and paintings.

Stieglitz and O'Keeffe were married on December 11, 1924. O'Keeffe was thirty-seven and Stieglitz almost sixty-one. In the early years of their relationship, O'Keeffe thought about the possibility of having children someday. Stieglitz, however, felt he was too old to start a new family. He wanted O'Keeffe to devote herself exclusively to her painting. O'Keeffe had always liked children, but she did see the conflict between raising a family and having enough time and energy to create art. She decided to go along with Stieglitz's feeling that she could not do both well.

O'Keeffe adopted Stieglitz's habit of living and working in New York City during the winter and spending the summer at Lake George. Beginning in the late nineteenth century, many American artists and writers had gone to live in Europe. "Not me," O'Keeffe said, "I had things to do in my own country."[6] O'Keeffe and Stieglitz never considered leaving the United States. Stieglitz's parents were born in Europe and he had been educated there, but he wanted to support a new artistic tradition that was all-American. O'Keeffe was born and educated in the United States. She was able to find what she needed for her painting in the American landscape.

Stieglitz and O'Keeffe lived in a series of rented apartments and ate their meals in neighborhood restaurants. They had very little money when they started out together. Stieglitz was always surrounded by talented artists and writers who enjoyed his company and conversation. With him, O'Keeffe lived in the center of the rich cultural life of New York, where she could hear nightly discussions of literature, art, music, and philosophy. O'Keeffe sat apart from these conversations, often sewing. She preferred solitude, but she listened and remembered what was useful and interesting to her.

Georgia O'Keeffe was the only woman in the small group of artists who were Stieglitz's closest friends and associates. "At first the men didn't want me around. They couldn't take a woman artist seriously," she said.[7] O'Keeffe had heard this sentiment before—from her older brother and from some of her fellow art students. She always resented the idea that she was referred to as a "woman painter" rather than simply a "painter."[8] O'Keeffe was not called "Mrs. Stieglitz." If someone addressed her that way, she would answer simply, "I am Georgia O'Keeffe."[9]

6

Flowers Larger
Than Life

"So I said to myself—I'll paint what I see."[1]

In 1925, O'Keeffe and Stieglitz moved into a new hotel in Manhattan. It was a modern brick skyscraper that O'Keeffe had watched go up. It towered over the surrounding buildings. They lived on the top floor of the thirty-story Shelton Hotel, high above the noise and congestion of the city. The Shelton was a residential hotel with dining rooms and lounges for all the residents to share. O'Keeffe's corner rooms had north-facing windows with good light for painting and a view of the East River.

In their new home, O'Keeffe devoted each day to painting as long as she had light from the windows. She kept her work area very clean and uncluttered. The walls were pale gray, and she covered the furniture with white cloths. She used a glass palette for her paints and a separate brush for each color. Keeping a careful record of the colors she used in each painting, she practiced different techniques as she worked.

The only bright colors in O'Keeffe's studio were in her pictures. The walls were usually bare except for whatever painting she was working on. "I like an empty wall," she said, "because I can imagine what I like on it."[2]

O'Keeffe had an exciting view of New York from her Shelton Hotel windows. Besides the rooftops of surrounding buildings, she could see the trees of Central Park, the cliffs of New Jersey across the Hudson River, the water traffic on the East River, and the smokestacks of factories on the other side. O'Keeffe could watch the sky by day and the brilliant lights of the city by night. She was especially interested in the other tall buildings rising on the Manhattan skyline— the seventy-seven-floor Chrysler Building and the American Radiator Building with its black brick and gold-leaf decoration.

O'Keeffe painted scenes of New York City while she lived there. Many are night scenes of tall buildings and the shimmering light after dark, without any people. When she first attempted to paint the city, Stieglitz and his male artist friends were skeptical about the subject matter for O'Keeffe, a country girl. However, when she exhibited her first city painting, *New York*, in her 1926 show, it sold the first day for $1,200. O'Keeffe had proved herself to the male artists. "From then on, they *let* me paint New York," she said.[3]

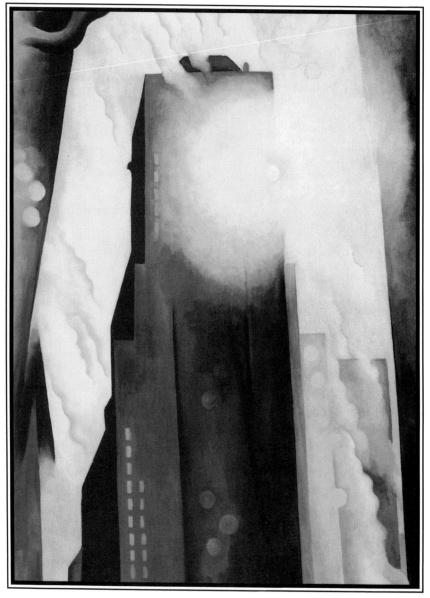

In 1926, O'Keeffe painted The Shelton with Sunspots *while living in this thirty-story hotel in Manhattan. It is oil on canvas, 123.2 x 76.8 centimeters (49 x 31 inches).*

O'Keeffe had always liked painting flowers, but in the 1920s she began a new series of flower pictures that would become some of her most famous works. She got the idea of painting a flower very close up and very large on the canvas. She explained that she wanted people to take time to really see the flower. "If I can paint that flower in a huge scale, then you could not ignore its beauty," she said.[4]

Her large-flower paintings were delicately colored and very detailed, almost like photographs. One art critic called them a bee's-eye view because they offer a very close-up look at the inside of the flowers.[5] O'Keeffe painted a wide variety of flowers—from the purple petunias she grew herself to the rare black irises she bought in a local flower shop.

O'Keeffe's pictures always stirred up notice among the art critics of New York. She usually tried not to be affected by criticism, especially if it made little sense to her. She often hung her paintings up together and assessed them for herself before they were publicly shown. After making her own judgment, she did not mind what other people thought or said about her work. "I have already settled it for myself," she wrote, "so flattery and criticism go down the same drain and I am quite free."[6]

Once she finished a group of paintings, she turned them over to Stieglitz for exhibit and sale. He set very high prices on her pictures because he wanted people to value them as much as he did. He sold only as many as were needed to pay the bills each year and only to people he thought would prize them. It was never easy or cheap to buy an O'Keeffe. Neither she nor Stieglitz really wanted to part with them.

By the end of the 1920s, Georgia O'Keeffe had become a painter who earned her living from her art. In the time since Stieglitz had gotten a loan for her to live and paint for a year, she had established her life as a working artist. Stieglitz had managed her career and publicity to allow her to thrive. After her 1928 show, Stieglitz reported that an anonymous art collector had offered the huge figure of $25,000 for six small calla lily paintings.

Stieglitz never offered proof of the sale, but newspapers printed his account of it. When the story of the sale appeared, O'Keeffe achieved a greater degree of fame than ever before. Stieglitz welcomed the public interest, and O'Keeffe got many requests for interviews. She told interviewers that she was simply practicing her art, not seeking fame and fortune.

From the time O'Keeffe first came to New York to live, she had accompanied Stieglitz every summer to his family's country home on the shores of Lake George. Although she enjoyed the beautiful country, the pine and birch woods and the lake, she liked it best in the quiet weeks before the rest of the Stieglitz relatives arrived and in the fall after they left.

As Stieglitz's wife, O'Keeffe had to take on some family and household responsibilities at the lake. She supervised the work of getting the house ready for summer visitors and preparing the meals. Stieglitz's sisters and brothers and their children and grandchildren came and went over the summer months. Sometimes family duties interfered with O'Keeffe's

Oriental Poppies, *1928, offered O'Keeffe's extraordinary close-up vision of flowers (oil on canvas, 30 x 40⅛ inches). She wanted viewers to be "surprised into taking time to look at it . . . to see what I see of flowers."*

solitary time for painting. In August 1926, she left the relatives at Lake George and went to the coast of Maine by herself to escape.

O'Keeffe had first visited the Maine sea coast in 1920. She walked along the beach and collected seaweed and shells for painting. She put them in a dish of seawater in her room to keep their colors fresh. Ocean scenery was a good break for her.

By the end of the 1920s, O'Keeffe began to feel she had painted all she could of the scenery around Lake George. "It was very pretty, but it wasn't made for me," she said.[7]

New Mexico

"I feel so alive that I am apt to crack at any moment."[1]

Georgia O'Keeffe's fame as a painter was growing. In 1927 the Brooklyn Museum devoted one room of its summer exhibition to her work. In 1929 she was invited to exhibit her work at New York's newly opened Museum of Modern Art. Her giant-flower paintings were very popular with the general public. Because of Stieglitz's careful management, Georgia O'Keeffe became both famous and wealthy—something not every working artist could achieve.[2]

In September 1928, Stieglitz began to have health problems. O'Keeffe did not paint much the following winter and had fewer new paintings than usual for her annual show in early 1929. She still dreamed of returning to the West, where she had been happy during her teaching days in Texas. Stieglitz had promised her that one day they would visit "her America" together.[3] At a time when many of their friends were taking vacations in New Mexico and other western states, it became less and less likely that Stieglitz would have the good health needed for traveling.

That winter in New York, O'Keeffe met some friends who lived in Taos, New Mexico. They invited her to come spend the summer with them. She began to think about the possibility of visiting New Mexico without Stieglitz. She had spent the previous eleven summers with him at Lake George. Stieglitz knew she was looking for new places to paint. Although he was not happy to be parted from O'Keeffe, he valued her art too much to ask that she not go. On April 27, 1929, at age forty-one, O'Keeffe left for New Mexico with her friend Rebecca Strand.

O'Keeffe and Beck Strand traveled by train to Santa Fe. O'Keeffe had first visited Santa Fe with her sister Claudia in 1917, and she found that it had not changed much. Located in the high-altitude foothills of the southern Rocky Mountains, Santa Fe was a gathering place for artists and craftsmen of three cultures. The historic town had been occupied for hundreds of years by Pueblo Indians, Spanish and Mexican colonists, and finally white settlers from the eastern United States. When O'Keeffe arrived, Santa Fe and Taos, seventy miles north, were beginning to attract tourists from all over the country.

O'Keeffe was less interested in the people of the area than in the land itself. What she saw in New Mexico pleased her very much. There was a great variety of landscape, from pine forests to desert sagebrush, from mountains to plains. The colors on the rocky cliffs changed with the hours of the day. The lack of moisture in the high desert air made everything look closer and brighter. "It's a different kind of color from any I'd ever seen," O'Keeffe said. "And it's not just the color that attracted me, either. The world is so wide up there, so big."[4]

O'Keeffe and Strand stayed at the home of Mabel Dodge Luhan in Taos. Luhan had moved to Taos from New York and loved to collect interesting and prominent people around her. She offered O'Keeffe a small adobe building surrounded by tall cottonwood trees to use as an art studio. The building had large windows and a beautiful view. O'Keeffe set up her easel and began to paint.

O'Keeffe stayed on in Taos until the end of August. She explored the countryside and met some of the other artists and writers who visited the Luhan home. Among them was a young man named Ansel Adams who was taking photographs for the Sierra Club.

She went on many camping trips with other guests that summer, by car and on horseback. One horseback trip took her to Kiowa Ranch, home of the English writer D. H. Lawrence and his wife, Frieda. The ranch buildings stood at an elevation of eight thousand feet in the mountains northwest of Taos. One night O'Keeffe lay on a bench under a tall pine tree and watched the stars move across the sky through its branches. She later painted a picture from that unique point of view and called it *D. H. Lawrence Pine Tree*. It was one of her favorite paintings.[5]

In Taos, O'Keeffe met photographer Ansel Adams, who became famous for his photographs of America's parks and wilderness areas. Behind Adams, above, is Moonrise, Hernandez, New Mexico, *one of his most popular pictures.*

O'Keeffe rode with friends on longer car trips, to the cliff dwellings of Mesa Verde in southern Colorado, the Canyon de Chelly of the Navajo Indians, and the Grand Canyon in Arizona. She toured the Indian pueblos in the area and one evening went to a rodeo. New experiences and new views of the world gave her ideas for painting.

That summer O'Keeffe decided to buy a car and learn to drive. She wanted to be able to explore the country on her own and to bring her painting gear along. She bought a black Model A Ford in Taos for $678. She named the car "Hello."

Paying for a car was no problem for O'Keeffe, but

learning how to drive was a difficult task. Her friends took turns helping her learn to operate the clutch and gearshift. The dirt roads of northern New Mexico were winding and narrow and full of rocky bumps. She wrote, "The bridges here are only wide enough for an angel to fly over so they give me great difficulty."[6]

When O'Keeffe left New Mexico in late August, she left the Model A with a friend in Taos. She shipped her summer paintings to New York, packed her trunk, and boarded the train for the East Coast. From the train, she wrote to a friend, "I have frozen in the mountains in rain and hail—and slept out under the stars—and cooked and burned on the desert . . . my nose has peeled and all my bones have been sore from riding— I even painted."[7]

She joined Stieglitz at Lake George on August 25 and was happily surprised. That summer, sixty-five-year-old Stieglitz was in improved health and had done some flying in a rented plane over the lake. O'Keeffe and Stieglitz were alone at Lake George in the peaceful fall season of 1929. O'Keeffe continued to work on some paintings she had brought from Taos and began new ones. As she and Stieglitz were preparing to return to New York City, the news was dark. In late October, the stock market began to fall, and soon the American economy would fall into the Great Depression.

Although the business climate was grim in New York, with many bankruptcies, Stieglitz went ahead with plans for O'Keeffe's annual winter exhibit. He rented space on the seventeenth floor of a modern office building on Madison Avenue. In December 1929, he opened his new gallery, An American Place.

Ansel Adams took this photo of Indian pueblos in Taos.

O'Keeffe designed the gallery, leaving the floors and windows bare. She painted the walls white.

In February 1930 her new exhibit opened. Most of the paintings on display were from her summer in New Mexico—the Taos Pueblo, the Mission Church at Ranchos de Taos, the black wooden crosses that dotted the New Mexico countryside. Art critics were startled by O'Keeffe's new subject matter. Some wrote favorable reviews and some did not. As usual, O'Keeffe made no plans to change her artistic views in reaction to anyone else's opinion. She had found a new world to explore with her art and resolved to return again the following summer to New Mexico.

Desert Bones

"My world is beautiful and impossible."[1]

For her second summer in New Mexico in 1930, O'Keeffe planned to be as independent as possible. She continued to work and sleep at Mabel Luhan's studio, but she ate in restaurants. She worked hard at her painting and maintained her solitude. "I don't need to see many people to live," she said.[2]

O'Keeffe began to collect the dry, sun-bleached bones of animals she found on her desert hikes. The bones were scattered over the New Mexico hills and plains—bones of cattle, horses, and sheep, animals that had been herded there for centuries. For O'Keeffe, the bones were not the remains of long-dead animals. They were interesting natural shapes, like the rocks and shells she had always collected. "The bones seem to cut sharply to the center of something that is keenly alive on the desert even tho' it is vast and empty and untouchable," she wrote.[3]

She decided to bring the bones with her when she returned east at the end of the summer. She packed them into a barrel, padded with fabric flowers she had bought from local craftsmen. The barrel of bones arrived safely in Lake George. O'Keeffe soon began to include the clean white shapes in her paintings.

Despite the bleak economic times, when almost ten million Americans had lost their jobs, O'Keeffe's paintings continued to sell very well at very good prices. They were being bought by museums, including the new Whitney Museum of American Art in New York. During the 1930s, her New Mexico paintings of hills, bones, wooden crosses, and adobe buildings were well received by the art world.

In the spring of 1931, O'Keeffe decided to go to New Mexico early, for May and June. She rented a cottage near the small town of Alcalde, in the Rio Grande Valley about forty miles south of Taos. There she found a new kind of landscape to explore and enjoy. She spent her mornings and evenings watching the dawn and the sunset from the roof of her cottage.

O'Keeffe took long drives into the dry plains, looking for interesting places to paint. Her Model A Ford was her studio on wheels. When she found a landscape she liked, she unfastened the driver's seat and turned it backward. She was able to paint while sitting inside the car. The car was tall enough to hold a 30-by-40-inch canvas, and the high windows let in plenty of light. "I think I never had a better time painting—and never worked more steadily and never loved the country more," she wrote.[4]

In mid-July, back at Lake George, she experimented with her animal bone paintings, adding artificial flowers and different colored backgrounds to the compositions. She worked hard until November and then took her thirty-three new paintings to New York to exhibit just before Christmas.

Once again, the art critics were amazed at O'Keeffe's latest creations. They had written about the symbolic meaning of her giant flowers in the 1920s. Now they were convinced that her bone and artificial flower pictures meant something, too. "The bones do not symbolize death," O'Keeffe protested. "They are shapes that I enjoy."[5]

Stieglitz began to have health problems once again, and O'Keeffe decided not to spend the summer of 1932 in New Mexico. Instead, the couple went to Lake George, where they found a good friend and companion in Stieglitz's twenty-seven-year-old niece, Georgia Engelhard. The lively younger Georgia enjoyed hiking, painting, and making fun of the other Stieglitz relatives. The two women decided to drive north together and visit the Gaspé Peninsula.

The trip to French Canada was O'Keeffe's first journey outside her own country. There she found more new subjects. She completed paintings of farm scenes, mountains, rugged sea coasts, and also the mariners' crosses that appeared at the water's edge. These crosses, different in design from the roadside crosses in New Mexico, were meant as memorials for sailors drowned at sea.

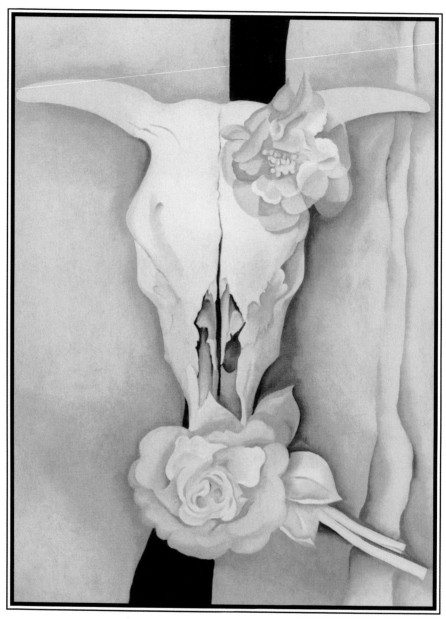

To O'Keeffe's eye, bones were living natural shapes. Her 1932 Cow's Skull with Calico Roses is oil on canvas, 92.2 x 61.3 centimeters (36 x 24 inches).

The Gaspé Peninsula had few places for tourists to eat and spend the night. The women found themselves asking for food and lodging in the homes of local farmers. The weather was very cold, in contrast to the desert heat that O'Keeffe usually enjoyed in the summer. Finally, she and her companion headed back to Lake George earlier than planned.

During the Depression, the United States government funded many works of public art, including murals on the walls of public buildings. O'Keeffe became interested in the idea of painting a mural—a very large scale picture. In 1932, she painted a design for a mural called *Manhattan* for an exhibit at the Museum of Modern Art.

After her work appeared in the museum exhibit, O'Keeffe was offered a job painting a mural for the new Radio City Music Hall being built at Rockefeller Center in New York. She would be paid $1,500, which was not unusual payment during the Depression era, but it was very low for the work of Georgia O'Keeffe. Stieglitz objected to the mural contract. He feared that working for so little would hurt the prices of her other paintings. O'Keeffe disagreed and insisted on going forward with the project.

Construction on the music hall moved slowly. O'Keeffe had made plans to begin work on the mural in August 1932, but the room it was planned for was still unfinished at the end of the summer. She would need at least ten weeks to complete the large project. In October, the canvas for painting was finally mounted on the walls. When O'Keeffe arrived to begin work, she found the canvas had been badly attached.

It was already beginning to peel away from the walls. She ran from the building in tears.

The time pressure, the poor quality of the surface she had to paint on, and Stieglitz's disapproval finally drove O'Keeffe to abandon the mural project. The failure of the project combined with the growing conflict in her marriage sent O'Keeffe into a period of depression and sickness. She was hospitalized on February 1, 1933. After a month and a half in the hospital, she began to recover. That spring she traveled to Bermuda with a friend. There she enjoyed the warm sun and the bright colors of the tropical island. As she began to feel better, she walked on the beach and collected shells.

In the summer O'Keeffe accompanied Stieglitz to Lake George. She still was not fully recovered from her illness and did very little painting during the rest of 1933. She spent the winter quietly at Lake George. In late January 1934, she went to New York to choose paintings for her annual exhibit. The exhibit would be a retrospective—a collection of her past work. It would feature her paintings done from 1915 to 1927.

O'Keeffe's annual exhibit in 1933 had attracted six thousand visitors. But in the depth of the Depression, none of the pictures had sold. Her 1934 exhibit, however, drew a crowd of seven thousand, and the paintings sold well.[6] In March, *Black Flower and Blue Larkspur*, one of O'Keeffe's New Mexico paintings, was purchased by the Metropolitan Museum of Art. It was her first sale to the Met, one of the world's most important museums.

As she emerged from her long months of illness, O'Keeffe had trouble recovering her energy and

O'Keeffe stands next to Cow's Skull—Red, White, and Blue, *which she painted in 1931 (oil on canvas, 40 x 36 inches).*

enthusiasm for painting. At the end of April she felt stronger and made plans to return at last to the Southwest. She left in June, inviting a friend to accompany her on the long drive. The past three years had been difficult ones, and O'Keeffe was ready for a fresh start on her life's work.

Not long after she arrived in northern New Mexico, O'Keeffe discovered Ghost Ranch and decided to make it her home. The country surrounding the ranch in the Rio Grande Valley gave her a new landscape to study. She spent the summer exploring the region and painting. The ranch made a very satisfactory home base for O'Keeffe. It was a comfortable center for her expeditions and the kind of dwelling place that gave her solitude, quiet, and constantly changing scenes of natural beauty.

Ladder to the Sky

"If you work hard enough, you can get almost anything."[1]

Once Georgia O'Keeffe found Ghost Ranch, she had a place to come back to each summer that suited her very well. The ranch was owned by Arthur Newton Pack, the publisher of *Nature* magazine who had moved to New Mexico from the East. Visitors came to the ranch to enjoy the wilderness, a place far from civilization and without telephones or electricity. Wild horses, mountain sheep, burros, deer, coyotes and rattlesnakes roamed the open land around the ranch.

O'Keeffe spent most of her time alone, hiking in the desert heat, cooling off in the small irrigation ditches, driving into distant canyons, and painting when she found a location she liked. She usually left the ranch at seven in the morning and returned about five in the afternoon. As she wandered, she collected the rocks, pieces of wood, and animal bones that interested her.

O'Keeffe tried to capture the colors she found in the rocks and hills in her paintings. She watched the colors change with the hours as clouds passed overhead and the sun moved across the sky. O'Keeffe painted the red hills around Ghost Ranch again and again. "A red hill doesn't touch everyone's heart as it touches mine," she said.[2] The wild empty country, often called wastelands or badlands, was for her the most beautiful country.[3]

Although there were many other visitors at Ghost Ranch, Georgia O'Keeffe kept to herself. Her friend the painter Dorothy Brett said about her, "When you got to know Georgia, she was a very, very nice person. But she had a rather cold front that made things a little difficult for her and for everybody else."[4]

O'Keeffe made at least one lifelong friend at the ranch and that was photographer Ansel Adams. She had met Adams in Taos on one of her earlier trips to New Mexico. He had also visited Stieglitz's gallery in New York. At Ghost Ranch, O'Keeffe lent Adams her car for his photography trips. One summer, she took a car trip with Adams and two other friends to explore western New Mexico and Arizona. O'Keeffe appears in many famous photographs taken by Ansel Adams. He said of her, "When Georgia O'Keeffe smiles, the whole world cracks open."[5]

While O'Keeffe spent her busy summers in New Mexico, Alfred Stieglitz remained in the East. O'Keeffe had hired a housekeeper to take care of him while she was away. Stieglitz had always encouraged Georgia to devote herself entirely to her artistic work. When her work took her away from him, he refused to complain. While O'Keeffe and Stieglitz were apart, they wrote letters to each other every day.

It was in the mid-1930s that O'Keeffe first met the famous American sculptor Alexander Calder. Soon after they met, Calder gave her a large decorative pin he had made from brass wire rolled into the letters *O* and *K*. Georgia O'Keeffe began wearing the O.K. initial pin all the time. Her friend Anita Pollitzer remembered it as the only piece of jewelry O'Keeffe ever wore.[6]

When O'Keeffe began her annual summer stays in New Mexico, her output of paintings increased. In 1936, she had seventeen new pictures to show, including the famous *Ram's Head, White Hollyhock, Hills*. In 1937, the year she would turn fifty, she had twenty new paintings in her yearly show. Pictures of animal bones suspended in the sky became regular features of her New Mexico work. *From the Faraway Nearby* portrayed a pair of elk antlers floating in a dawn sky with mountains.

When O'Keeffe returned to Ghost Ranch in July 1937, she found to her surprise that there was no room for her. She had made her plans at the last minute and had not notified owner Arthur Pack that she would be coming. Pack had a small house three miles from ranch headquarters that he had built for his family but was not using. He offered to let her stay there. O'Keeffe agreed. She loved the house at first sight. "As soon as I saw it, I knew I must have it," she

O'Keeffe treasured the "O.K." pin sculpted for her by Alexander Calder.

said. "I can't understand people who want something badly but don't grab for it. I grabbed."[7]

The adobe house, made of mud and straw bricks, was called Rancho de los Burros. Arthur Pack had chosen the site for the house because it had an excellent view of Pedernal Mountain, a flat-topped mesa about ten miles to the south. *Pedernal* means "flint" in Spanish. The native people had gathered flint there to use for arrowheads.

O'Keeffe painted a series of pictures of the Pedernal that summer. Over the years, the mountain appeared again and again in her work. O'Keeffe said about the Pedernal, "God told me if I painted that mountain enough, he'd give it to me."[8]

The view of the Pedernal was only one attraction of the new house. Like many adobe houses in the Southwest, Rancho de los Burros had a flat roof that served as an extra room. A rough wooden ladder made of straight slender tree trunks rested against the outside wall of the house. When O'Keeffe climbed the ladder, she could stand on the roof and see the great cliffs to the north. The cliffs, almost seven hundred feet high, were made of layers of ancient rock. The bottom layer of red rock, two hundred million years old, was followed by a middle layer of yellow sandstone and a top layer of gray gypsum and limestone.

O'Keeffe spent the summer at the Rancho de los Burros house with a housekeeper to help her. She climbed the ladder to the roof in the evening to watch the sunset and then the nighttime stars. In later years at the house, she slept on the roof in a sleeping bag so that she could watch the stars and the sunrise.

Two special paintings from that summer are *My Backyard*, a desert landscape, and *The House I Live In*, the ranch with the Pedernal in the background.

During the 1930s Georgia O'Keeffe's art shows at An American Place brought in large crowds. She was popular not only with those who knew art and collected it, but also with the general public. In 1938, *Life* magazine did a photo story about her. When she went to an auto repair shop in New York to pick up her car, the mechanic recognized her name. He told her that he had cut out a picture of her painting of a horse's skull from the *Life* article and put it on the wall in his living room.[9]

In the spring of 1938, O'Keeffe went back to Williamsburg, Virginia, with three of her sisters. She was being given an honorary doctorate of fine arts from the College of William and Mary. O'Keeffe was pleased to accept the honor. It was the only degree she had besides her high school diploma. The next year she was named one of the twelve most outstanding women of the past fifty years by a committee of the New York World's Fair. Her painting *Sunset, Long Island* was selected to represent New York State at the fair. By the end of the 1930s, Georgia O'Keeffe was the most famous and most successful woman painter in the United States.[10]

O'Keeffe achieved her dream of buying the Rancho de los Burros house at Ghost Ranch in the summer of 1940. She was fifty-two years old, and it was the first home she had ever owned. In New York she had lived in rented apartments in the city and the Stieglitz family

74

From the Rancho de los Burros, O'Keeffe could see the flat-topped Pedernal Mountain. "God told me if I painted that mountain enough, he'd give it to me," she said.

home at Lake George. The Ghost Ranch house was hers to return to whenever she wanted.

Even though O'Keeffe loved the beauty and the isolation of her house at Ghost Ranch, it was not easy to live there. She had no running water or electricity in the house. She could not plant a garden in the rocky desert soil. Food stores were miles away over rough country roads. Living so far from civilization was risky, but Georgia O'Keeffe was always willing to takes chances for her work.

O'Keeffe wanted to keep as much time as possible free for painting, so she usually had a housekeeper who lived with her in the summer to take care of the work around the house. One woman who spent many summers with her was Maria Chabot. Not only did Chabot help around the house, she also took camping trips with O'Keeffe and helped her get to distant wilderness places where she could paint. Two of O'Keeffe's favorite painting places, which she called the White Place and the Black Place, were remote locations where she and Chabot camped overnight.

O'Keeffe chose these names because of the colors of the rocks. White Place, south of Ghost Ranch, was a formation of white volcanic ash. Black Place was in Navajo country north of Ghost Ranch. "It looks like a mile of elephants—grey hills all about the same size," she wrote.[11] O'Keeffe painted in the heat of the summer sun and in the high wind that often blew in the desert. She endured the cold and the rain to get to the places she wanted to paint.

During the years that the United States was involved in World War II, 1941 to 1945, O'Keeffe continued to spend the summers in her house at Ghost Ranch. In 1942, the Art Institute of Chicago, where she had studied in 1905, offered to hold the first big retrospective art show of her career. A retrospective exhibit would bring together Georgia O'Keeffe paintings from past years so they could be viewed and enjoyed as a group. O'Keeffe had not yet had a large exhibit outside of An American Place, where Stieglitz had been showing her new work every year.

The exhibit opened on January 31, 1943. The sixty-one paintings represented more than twenty-five years' worth of pictures—flowers and fruit, landscapes and bones. The oldest was a charcoal drawing from

1915, and the newest was *Turkey Feathers and Indian Pot* from 1941.

Art critics offered their usual mixed response. Some liked what they saw, and some did not. O'Keeffe herself was confident and pleased with her work. Her enjoyment of creating art helped her ignore any negative criticism. As she said to an art critic in New York, "I still like the way I see things best."[12]

A Change of Life

"A great sorrow is a great experience . . . but I can not help feeling that a great joy is more to my liking."[1]

Fourteen miles south of Ghost Ranch, not far from O'Keeffe's White Place, was the tiny village of Abiquiu (a-bee-cue). O'Keeffe had visited it in her early explorations of the area. There she saw the ruins of an abandoned hacienda that local people called "the Chavez property." She had climbed through a broken section of the adobe wall that surrounded it and found the remains of a large garden. The old hacienda sat on a hilltop overlooking the green Chama River Valley. O'Keeffe remembered the place and had a chance to buy it in December 1945. She wanted the property because it had water for irrigation and good soil for growing vegetables.

The Abiquiu house needed much work to make it livable. New adobe bricks were made for an addition

O'Keeffe trims a plant on her patio at Abiquiu.

to the house. Walls were opened up to make room for new and larger windows. O'Keeffe wanted to add a fireplace in every room. Local workers mixed and applied pink-brown mud to the outside adobe walls by hand. The restoration was not finished until 1948. From her new home, O'Keeffe could see the cotton-wood trees along the Chama River and the distant mesas and mountains on the horizon.

During the early 1940s, O'Keeffe spent only about four months a year in New York. She spent the winter months with Stieglitz and prepared for her annual exhibit of new paintings. Stieglitz turned eighty in 1944, and his health was growing worse. O'Keeffe's spring departures for New Mexico were hard for both of them. Stieglitz was dedicated to O'Keeffe's well-being, though. He knew that her life in New Mexico made her happy, and happiness enabled her to paint.

In May 1946, O'Keeffe had another major retro-spective, this time at the Museum of Modern Art in New York. It was the first such show for a woman at the museum since it had opened in 1929. Fifty-seven of her pictures from 1915 to 1945 were on display just a block and a half from Stieglitz's small gallery, An American Place.

O'Keeffe left early the next month for New Mexico, flying there for the first time. A month later, she was out driving when a boy with a telegram waved at her to stop. The telegram was from New York, telling her that Stieglitz had had a stroke and was in critical condition. O'Keeffe drove straight to the airport in Albuquerque and caught a plane for New York. There, she found

Stieglitz in a coma with little chance of recovery. He died in the early morning of July 13, 1946.

O'Keeffe carried out Stieglitz's wishes after his death. She found a simple pine coffin for him and sat up late into the night, removing the coffin's pink satin lining and replacing it with plain white linen. Stieglitz had asked that there be no words spoken and no music played at his memorial service. After a small group of mourners quietly paid tribute, O'Keeffe accompanied the coffin to a crematorium in Queens, New York. Later she took the ashes to Lake George, where she buried them at the foot of a pine tree beside the lake.

O'Keeffe spent the autumn in Abiquiu. She returned to New York in late November to begin the enormous job of preserving Stieglitz's legacy. O'Keeffe had inherited the task of finding homes for his lifetime collection of modern paintings and sculpture by many American artists, his papers, and his own photographic works.

Stieglitz and O'Keeffe had talked about where to place his collection. Stieglitz thought everything should be kept together. O'Keeffe decided it would be better to divide the materials among many museums and universities.

During the three winters from 1946 to 1949, O'Keeffe worked at the overwhelming job of cataloging and giving away eight hundred fifty works of modern art, hundreds of photographs, and fifty thousand letters. The largest share of the art went to the Metropolitan Museum in New York, the second largest to the Art Institute of Chicago. Yale University received Stieglitz's letters and other papers. When she had finished settling the estate, O'Keeffe moved permanently to New Mexico.

O'Keeffe had continued to spend her summers in New Mexico during the years that she worked on Stieglitz's collections. In the summer of 1947, dinosaur bones were discovered at Ghost Ranch, bringing many tourists, scientists, and reporters to the area. O'Keeffe got little painting done that season. The summer of 1948 was more productive. Heavy rain during the spring had made the desert bloom, giving her more opportunities to paint desert flowers, like the yucca, that seldom blossomed.

Georgia O'Keeffe was sixty-one years old in the spring of 1949 when she gave up her New York apartment and settled permanently in New Mexico. She went into a quiet period when her art was not as popular or as much in the public eye as it had been. Without Stieglitz to keep her in the spotlight, she moved into a life of greater solitude and privacy.

When O'Keeffe began spending her winters in New Mexico, she discovered a new season of light and color. She lived at Abiquiu during the winter because it was more protected from the weather and less isolated than Ghost Ranch. To keep warm, O'Keeffe burned spicy piñon wood from the nearby mountains in her fireplace. She wrote to her friend Anita Pollitzer: "The world is big and wide and wonderful even if the life is hard."[2]

O'Keeffe followed a painting rhythm that depended on finding inspiration and then planning her work carefully before beginning. "I know what I'm going to do before I begin, and if there's nothing in my head, I

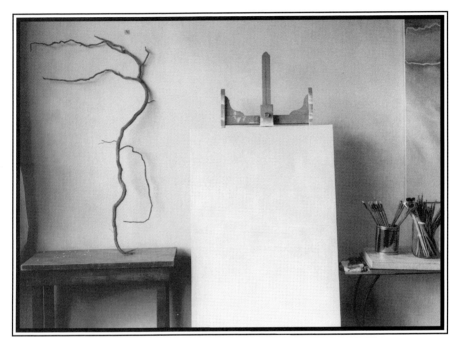

O'Keeffe kept her studio spare at Abiquiu. The only bright colors were in her pictures.

do nothing," she said.[3] Sometimes she went weeks or months without picking up a brush until the right idea came to her. "I get this shape in my head," she said. "My mind creates shapes."[4]

Although she led an isolated life in New Mexico, O'Keeffe always had household help. Then at Christmas in 1952, a friend gave her two Chinese chow puppies. The fluffy puppies, Bo and Chia, were intended as watchdogs, but as they grew, they became her much-loved pets.[5] They followed her everywhere. After her first two chows died, she raised two more pairs during her long life.

Now that she lived in New Mexico year-round, O'Keeffe planted a large garden at Abiquiu. It provided vegetables for her meals. She also planted almond and mulberry trees for shade and an orchard of apricot, peach, and apple trees. Winter and spring were spent at Abiquiu; in the summer and autumn she lived fourteen miles north at Ghost Ranch.

During the 1950s, O'Keeffe saw many changes in her corner of rural New Mexico. Increasing numbers of cars, trucks, airplanes, and tourists began to appear in her once isolated valley. The main buildings and property of Ghost Ranch were donated to the Presbyterian Church for a conference center. The road to the ranch was paved, and electricity and telephones were installed.

As modern civilization arrived in northern New Mexico, Georgia O'Keeffe began to move out into the world herself. In 1951, when she was sixty-three, she took a long driving trip to Mexico with friends. They visited Mexico City, Cuernavaca, Oaxaca, Guadalajara, and the Yucatán Peninsula. O'Keeffe met the famous Mexican mural painter Diego Rivera and his wife, Frida Kahlo, also an artist. To bring the bright colors of Mexico home with her, O'Keeffe bought pottery, baskets, blankets, and other handicrafts.

On the same trip, O'Keeffe and her friends also visited Big Bend National Park in south Texas and Carlsbad Caverns in southern New Mexico. In all, they drove five thousand miles in six weeks. For O'Keeffe, it was the beginning of a decade of travel that would eventually take her around the world.

Ageless Beauty

"I think more about tomorrow than today or yesterday."[1]

In the spring of 1953, when O'Keeffe was sixty-five years old, she took her first trip to Europe. She toured France, seeing the great works of art. She thought the country was beautiful, but told her friends that she preferred her American homeland.[2] She enjoyed Spain so much that she returned the following summer and stayed for three weeks. She liked the Spanish painters whose work she saw in Madrid—El Greco, Velázquez, and Goya. She also took pleasure in the culture of Spain, especially the bullfights.

When she was seventy-one, O'Keeffe made a three-and-a-half-month trip around the world. Starting in San Francisco, she flew west to Asia. She had admired Asian art since her early student days, when her teacher Arthur Wesley Dow had shown his large collection of Japanese prints. O'Keeffe liked Chinese painting, which she believed was the best in the world.[3]

From the Far East—Tokyo, Hong Kong, and Taiwan—O'Keeffe traveled to Southeast Asia, India, the Middle East, and western Europe. The following year she returned to Japan and Cambodia to see things she had missed. Once she felt satisfied that she had seen the world, she told people that she knew she lived in the right place. Of her home in New Mexico, she said, "I don't think there's anything as good as this."[4]

During the decade after Stieglitz's death, O'Keeffe lived quietly, traveled, and did not show her paintings. Then, in 1960, she was invited to exhibit her work at the Worcester Art Museum in Massachusetts. It would be her first major exhibition in fourteen years. For O'Keeffe, it meant a lot of hard work: framing new pictures, packing and shipping them, and arranging the paintings on the museum walls. She did most of the work herself because the presentation of her paintings was part of her artistry.

Daniel Catton Rich, the director of the Worcester Art Museum, knew Georgia O'Keeffe's work well. He had first met her in Taos in 1929 and had been the curator of her exhibit at the Art Institute of Chicago in 1943. The new Worcester exhibit spanned forty years of O'Keeffe paintings and included some new ones of desert rivers seen from the air. For the catalog of the 1960 exhibition, Rich wrote, "At seventy-two, O'Keeffe can still surprise herself. I have a feeling that she will continue to surprise all of us for quite some time to come."[5]

The Worcester exhibit brought Georgia O'Keeffe and her work back into the public eye. Interviews and stories about her appeared in national magazines with color photographs of her work. She was once again visible to the world. A new generation of artists and art lovers began to know and appreciate her. In the summer of 1961, the photo magazine *Look* featured O'Keeffe in a story called "Ageless Beauties." In 1962, she was elected to the American Academy of Arts and Letters, the nation's highest honor for people in the arts.

Later that summer O'Keeffe took a raft trip through Glen Canyon on the upper Colorado River. She was seventy-three years old when she embarked on this 185-mile adventure, paddling on the river by day and sleeping on sandbars under the stars at night. She insisted on doing everything for herself on the ten-day trip, just like the younger members of the expedition. She said, "If I can't do it myself, I shouldn't be on the trip."[6]

Georgia O'Keeffe had been a painter of the land and the sky since her early days in Canyon, Texas. When she began to see the sky from an airplane, she used that new point of view for some of her most remarkable work. In 1965 she began the largest painting of her career—twenty-four feet long and eight feet high. She mounted a huge roll of canvas on the inside wall of the garage at Ghost Ranch. From early June, she painted steadily all summer. She stood on a table to paint the top of the canvas. She sat on the floor to paint the bottom. *Sky Above Clouds IV* featured a vast blue sky with soft, white, oval clouds floating in rows.

After a long day of painting, O'Keeffe would climb a small hill behind her house and look back at the painting through the open garage door. The rays of the setting sun would shine on the painting, making a patch of blue glow in the fading light. O'Keeffe finished the painting in time for the largest show of her work ever to be held. In the spring of 1966, the huge canvas traveled with ninety-five other paintings to the Amon Carter Museum of Western Art in Fort Worth, Texas.

In the fall of 1970, Georgia O'Keeffe had a retrospective at the Whitney Museum of American Art—her first major show in New York since Stieglitz's death twenty-four years earlier. The retrospective drew immense crowds in New York, and later in Chicago and San Francisco. Many in the younger generation were seeing the work of Georgia O'Keeffe for the first time and found something they liked. "It was astonishing to me the way young people responded to it," she said.[7] The artist, now in her eighties, could speak to all generations. Her popularity placed her once again in the center of the modern art world.

Still, time was beginning to affect O'Keeffe's life. When she was eighty-three, she realized she had lost part of her eyesight. She could no longer see clearly from the center of her eyes. Her peripheral vision—around the edges—was fine, but her always sharp gray-green eyes were failing. She went to many eye doctors, but there was nothing they could do.

One day in the late autumn of 1973, when Georgia O'Keeffe was eighty-six years old, a young handyman came to her door looking for work. O'Keeffe offered Juan Hamilton the job of packing some paintings for shipping. This began a friendship between them that lasted for the rest of her life.

O'Keeffe discovered that Hamilton was trained as

O'Keeffe was photographed at her 1970 retrospective at the Whitney Museum of American Art. The exhibit featured 121 of her paintings, watercolors, and drawings.

a potter, and she encouraged him to work at his art, making clay pots on her kitchen table. Hamilton suggested that O'Keeffe herself try working with clay because her failing vision was making it difficult for her to paint. She tried making pots from rolled coils of clay but was never quite satisfied with the results: "I cannot yet make the clay speak."[8]

Eventually, with encouragement from Hamilton and other friends, she returned to painting, doing the best she could to work despite her vision problems. On a trip to Washington, D.C., she spent some time looking at the Washington Monument and was inspired to create a series of paintings called *From a Day with Juan*. Her cloudy vision even gave her new ways of seeing shapes and colors. Sometimes she used binoculars and a magnifying glass to help her complete a project.

Juan Hamilton served as O'Keeffe's assistant and encouraged her to respond to requests for information about her life and work. With his help, it was easier to make herself more available to those who admired her painting and wanted to know more about her career and her development as an artist.

O'Keeffe agreed to write a book about her life and how her paintings were created. *Georgia O'Keeffe*, by Georgia O'Keeffe, appeared in the fall of 1976. It contained more than a hundred pictures and opened to an usual width of two feet. According to Hamilton, the book was not exactly a life story. "It's about the pictures," said O'Keeffe.[9]

While O'Keeffe was at work on the book, she allowed a television crew to come to Ghost Ranch and

Abiquiu to film her at home. The documentary featured O'Keeffe and Hamilton talking about her life and work. It was shown on television to celebrate O'Keeffe's ninetieth birthday in November 1977.

Her successful book and the documentary brought public attention to O'Keeffe once again. Large stacks of mail poured in from museums, schools, historians, art dealers, and art lovers. Requests for interviews and photographs came daily, and more invitations to receive awards and honorary degrees came with each passing year.

With increasing fame, O'Keeffe's wealth also increased. She had always been very successful financially. From her early sales in the 1920s, the prices of her pictures continued to climb. In 1985 her painting *White Rose—New Mexico* was sold at auction for more than $1,250,000.

In her nineties, O'Keeffe continued to live her quiet, steady life. She woke up at dawn, did exercises, had breakfast, and walked with her dogs. She went to bed at sundown, listened as her housekeeper read to her, and rested just a few hours a night. With all that she had accomplished in life, she never lost interest in the coming of a new day. "I always wanted to be five or six of me," she said.[10]

O'Keeffe traced her success in life to her ability to know what she wanted and to work hard for it. She knew that she wanted to paint, so she built her life around her art. "I've been very lucky," she said. But she made much of her own luck with courage and dedication. She took many chances. "My life is like

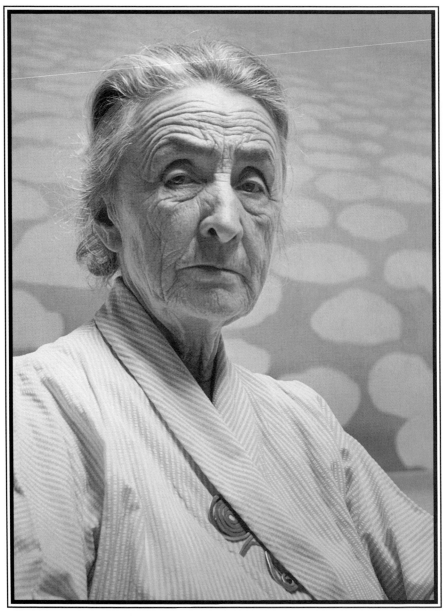

O'Keeffe poses in front of Sky Above Clouds II, *1963 (43 x 83 inches), one of a series of paintings of soft, floating clouds.*

walking on a knife's edge, but I would do it again. I [was] doing something I really liked to do."[11]

O'Keeffe stayed on at Ghost Ranch. "Living out here has just meant happiness," she said.[12] She told people she planned to live to be one hundred. "I don't think she was ever concerned about death because I don't think she ever thought she would die," wrote Juan Hamilton.[13] In the years approaching her one hundredth birthday, she helped make plans for a centennial exhibit of her work at the National Gallery of Art in Washington, D.C.

In her late nineties, O'Keeffe had to move to Santa Fe to be closer to medical care. On March 6, 1986, she died at Saint Vincent's Hospital. She was ninety-eight. At her request, no funeral or memorial service was held. Her body was cremated and her ashes scattered on Pedernal Mountain near Ghost Ranch. "When I think of death," she had said, "I only regret that I will not be able to see this beautiful country anymore, unless the Indians are right and my spirit will walk here after I'm gone."[14]

Georgia O'Keeffe's Legacy

"No less than her paintings, her life was a work of art."[1]

The life and the work of Georgia O'Keeffe were both considered front-page news at the time of her death in 1986. *The New York Times* called her a "key figure in the American 20th century."[2] Art critic John Russell wrote, "It would be difficult to imagine American painting in the first half of this [the twentieth] century without the presence of Georgia O'Keeffe."[3]

Born on a midwestern farm and trained in American schools, O'Keeffe considered herself an all-American artist. "I think that what I have done is something rather unique in my time and that I am one of the few who give our country any voice of its own," she wrote.[4] Alfred Stieglitz agreed that O'Keeffe's art "could only have come from a woman and from America."[5]

When O'Keeffe was free to choose a home for herself, she moved to a spot in the desert where the land could be her main subject. A friend said O'Keeffe was seeking the "wonderful part of America that city people, who talk of an American art, forget."[6] The works of Georgia O'Keeffe are recognized not only in the United States but around the world. Historian Robert Hughes called her "the most famous woman artist America ever produced."[7]

When O'Keeffe began her career as a painter, few American women were attempting to work as professional artists. O'Keeffe broke away from art traditions of the past and developed her own original style and standard of beauty. She set an example of independent thinking, risk taking, and courage. "She raised the awareness of the American public to the fact that a woman could be the equal of any man in her chosen field," said art critic Edith Evans Asbury.[8]

O'Keeffe painted to please herself, but she pleased the world as well. In July 1997, the Georgia O'Keeffe Museum opened in Santa Fe, New Mexico. Since it opened, more than eight hundred thousand people have visited the remodeled Spanish Baptist Mission to see the largest Georgia O'Keeffe collection in the world.[9] "O'Keeffe's legacy is one whose impact will be felt for years to come. The broad range of her artistic output and its appeal to an equally wide audience, for young people and adult viewers alike, demonstrates this artist's unique aesthetic qualities," said museum director George King.[10]

From the first showing of her pictures in New York in 1916 to her final years in New Mexico in the 1980s,

O'Keeffe considered herself an all-American artist. In her lifetime, she created two thousand paintings, drawings, and sculptures.

Georgia O'Keeffe brought her special world to life for all to see. She worked to translate the shape of her experience into painted forms. "I have picked flowers . . . ," she wrote, "picked up sea shells and rocks and pieces of wood. . . . When I found the beautiful white bones on the desert I picked them up. . . . I have used these things to say what is to me the wideness and wonder of the world as I live in it."[11]

When she was eighty-six, Georgia O'Keeffe told an interviewer that three pieces of good luck had shaped her life. First, she had met Alfred Stieglitz, the champion of modern American artists. Second, she had traveled to the high plains of Texas, where vast open spaces gave her art new life. Third, she had discovered Ghost Ranch, her beloved New Mexican home, where things were always beautiful, interesting, and a little mysterious.[12] In describing her life's good luck, Georgia O'Keeffe also added that hard work and courage mattered, too. "I'm frightened all the time," she said. "But I've never let it stop me. Never!"[13]

Her originality and her independence made Georgia O'Keeffe one of a kind. As Ansel Adams said, "She's just O'Keeffe. She wears a certain kind of clothes, has a certain manner. She's a very great artist. Nobody can look at a painting without being deeply affected. So the mystique begins and endures."[14] Prominent art historian Barbara Rose called her "a surprisingly small woman who was always larger than life. . . . There will never be another Georgia O'Keeffe."[15]

Chronology

1887—Born near Sun Prairie, Wisconsin, on November 15.

1903—Moves to Williamsburg, Virginia. Attends Chatham Episcopal Institute.

1905—Studies at the Art Institute of Chicago with
-1906   John Vanderpoel.

1907—Studies at the Art Students League, New York,
-1908   with William Merritt Chase; visits exhibits of modern art at Alfred Stieglitz's 291 Gallery.

1908—Works as a commercial artist in Chicago.
-1910

1912—Attends summer art classes taught by Alon Bement at the University of Virginia.

1912—Teaches art and penmanship in public schools
-1914   in Amarillo, Texas.

1914—Studies at Columbia University's Teachers
-1915   College, New York, with Arthur Wesley Dow.

1915—Teaches art at Columbia College, Columbia,
-1916   South Carolina.

1916—Begins teaching art at West Texas State Normal College in Canyon.

1917—Stieglitz presents O'Keeffe's first solo exhibit at 291 Fifth Avenue; in the summer, makes first visit to New Mexico.

1918—Moves to New York in June to begin career as a professional artist.

1923—Stieglitz exhibits one hundred O'Keeffe works at the Anderson Galleries.

1924—Marries Alfred Stieglitz on December 11.

1928—Stieglitz announces sale of six calla lily paintings for a record price ($25,000).

1929—Spends first summer in New Mexico.

1933—Hospitalized in New York for nervous exhaustion.

1934—Returns to New Mexico after three years; makes first visit to Ghost Ranch.

1938—Receives honorary degree from the College of William and Mary, the first of many such honors.

1939—Honored as one of twelve outstanding women of the past fifty years by a World's Fair committee.

1940—Buys house at Ghost Ranch.

1943—The Art Institute of Chicago presents the first complete retrospective of O'Keeffe's work.

1945—Buys abandoned house in Abiquiu to remodel for winter home.

1946—Is first woman to be honored with retrospective at New York's Museum of Modern Art; Stieglitz dies on July 13.

1946—Works in New York to settle Stieglitz's estate.
–1949

1949—In June, moves permanently to New Mexico.

1953—Makes first trip to Europe.

1959—Spends three and a half months traveling around the world.

1962—Elected to American Academy of Arts and Letters.

1970—Whitney Museum of American Art in New York presents O'Keeffe retrospective, which later travels to Chicago and New York; eyesight begins to fail.

1973—Meets Juan Hamilton, who becomes her assistant.

1976—Publishes *Georgia O'Keeffe*, the story of her paintings.

1977—Television film *Georgia O'Keeffe* airs for the first time for her ninetieth birthday celebration.

1986—Dies in Santa Fe, New Mexico, on March 6.

1987—National Gallery of Art in Washington, D.C., celebrates the one hundredth year of O'Keeffe's birth with retrospective exhibit that later travels to Chicago, Dallas, New York, and Los Angeles.

1997—Georgia O'Keeffe Museum opens in Santa Fe, New Mexico.

Chapter 1. The Search for Ghost Ranch

1. Laurie Lisle, *Portrait of an Artist: A Biography of Georgia O'Keeffe* (New York: Washington Square Press, 1986), p. 227.

2. Ibid., p. 270.

3. Roxana Robinson, *Georgia O'Keeffe: A Life* (New York: Harper & Row, 1989), p. 408.

4. Calvin Tomkins, "Georgia O'Keeffe—The Rose in the Eye Looked Pretty Fine," *The New Yorker*, March 4, 1974, p. 40.

5. Robinson, p. 407.

6. Ibid., p. 448.

7. Leo Janos, "Georgia O'Keeffe at Eighty-Four," *Atlantic Monthly*, December, 1971, p. 117.

Chapter 2. Sun Prairie Days

1. Calvin Tomkins, "Georgia O'Keeffe—The Rose in the Eye Looked Pretty Fine," *The New Yorker*, March 4, 1974, p. 41.

2. Georgia O'Keeffe, *Georgia O'Keeffe* (New York: Viking, 1976), pages unnumbered.

3. Roxana Robinson, *Georgia O'Keeffe: A Life* (New York: Harper & Row, 1989), p. 21.

4. Anita Pollitzer, *A Woman on Paper: Georgia O'Keeffe* (New York: Simon & Schuster, 1988), p. 62.

5. O'Keeffe, pages unnumbered.

6. Ibid.

7. Robinson, p. 30.

8. O'Keeffe, pages unnumbered.

9. *Georgia O'Keeffe*, video, producer/director Perry Miller Adato, WNET/13 (Chicago: Home Vision, 1977).

10. Robinson, p. 31.

11. O'Keeffe, pages unnumbered.

12. Ibid.

Chapter 3. An Artist's Education

1. *Georgia O'Keeffe*, video, producer/director Perry Miller Adato, WNET/13 (Chicago: Home Vision, 1977).

2. Laurie Lisle, *Portrait of an Artist: A Biography of Georgia O'Keeffe* (New York: Washington Square Press, 1986), pp. 31–32.

3. Roxana Robinson, *Georgia O'Keeffe: A Life* (New York: Harper & Row, 1989), p. 41.

4. Ibid., p. 45.

5. Lisle, p. 33.

6. Robinson, p. 45.

7. Calvin Tomkins, "Georgia O'Keeffe—The Rose in the Eye Looked Pretty Fine," *The New Yorker*, March 4, 1974, p. 41.

8. Georgia O'Keeffe, *Georgia O'Keeffe* (New York: Viking, 1976), pages unnumbered.

9. Lisle, p. 41.

10. Ibid., p. 43.

11. O'Keeffe, pages unnumbered.

12. Ralph Looney, "Georgia O'Keeffe," *Atlantic Monthly*, April 1965, p. 107.

13. Anita Pollitzer, *A Woman on Paper: Georgia O'Keeffe* (New York: Simon & Schuster, 1988), p. 101.

14. Ibid., p. 100.

15. Lisle, p. 53.

16. Mary Lynn Kotz, "A Day with Georgia O'Keeffe," *Art News*, December, 1977, p. 37.

17. Lisle, p. 59.

Chapter 4. Teaching Art

1. Jack Cowart, Juan Hamilton, and Sarah Greenough, *Georgia O'Keeffe: Art and Letters* (Boston: New York Graphic Society/Little, Brown, 1987), p. 189.

2. Calvin Tomkins, "Georgia O'Keeffe—The Rose in the Eye Looked Pretty Fine," *The New Yorker*, March 4, 1974, p. 41.

3. Roxana Robinson, *Georgia O'Keeffe: A Life* (New York: Harper & Row, 1989), p. 90.

4. Anita Pollitzer, *A Woman on Paper: Georgia O'Keeffe* (New York: Simon & Schuster, 1988) p. 108.

5. Ibid., p. 2.

6. Laurie Lisle, *Portrait of an Artist: A Biography of Georgia O'Keeffe* (New York: Washington Square Press, 1986), p. 70.

7. Ibid., pp. 72–73.

8. Ralph Looney, "Georgia O'Keeffe," *Atlantic Monthly*, April 1965, p. 107.

9. Pollitzer, p. 120.

10. Mitchell A. Wilder, editor, *Georgia O'Keeffe: An Exhibition of the Work of the Artist from 1915 to 1966* (Fort Worth, Tex.: Amon Carter Museum of Western Art, 1966), p. 10.

11. Looney, p. 107.

12. Georgia O'Keeffe, *Georgia O'Keeffe* (New York: Viking, 1976), pages unnumbered.

13. Anita Pollitzer, "That's Georgia," *Saturday Review*, November 4, 1950, p. 42.

14. Pollitzer, *A Woman on Paper*, p. 120.

15. N. Heller and J. Williams, "Georgia O'Keeffe: The American Southwest," *American Artist*, January 1976, p. 81.

16. Lisle, p. 94.

17. Ibid., p. 102.

18. Pollitzer, "That's Georgia," p. 42.

Chapter 5. Stieglitz and New York

1. Georgia O'Keeffe, *Georgia O'Keeffe* (New York: Viking, 1976), pages unnumbered.

2. Rhoda Barkan and Peter Sinclaire, *From Santa Fe to O'Keeffe Country: A One-Day Journey Through the Soul of New Mexico* (Santa Fe, N.M.: Ocean Tree Books, 1996), p. 73.

3. Anita Pollitzer, *A Woman on Paper: Georgia O'Keeffe* (New York: Simon & Schuster, 1988), p. 208.

4. *Georgia O'Keeffe*, video, producer/director Perry Miller Adato, WNET/13 (Chicago: Home Vision, 1977).

5. Laurie Lisle, *Portrait of an Artist: A Biography of Georgia O'Keeffe* (New York: Washington Square Press, 1986), p. 134.

6. Edith Evans Asbury, "Silent Desert Still Charms Georgia O'Keeffe, Near 81," *The New York Times*, November 2, 1968, p. L 39.

7. Dorothy Seiberling, "A Flowering in the Stieglitz Years," *Life*, March 1, 1968, p. 52.

8. Barbara Rose, "Georgia O'Keeffe, 1887–1986," *Vogue*, May 1986, p. 292.

9. Lisle, p. 158.

Chapter 6. Flowers Larger Than Life

1. Georgia O'Keeffe, *Georgia O'Keeffe* (New York: Viking, 1976), pages unnumbered.

2. Anita Pollitzer, "That's Georgia," *Saturday Review*, November 4, 1950, p. 43.

3. Ralph Looney, "Georgia O'Keeffe," *Atlantic Monthly*, April 1965, p. 108.

4. Mary Lynn Kotz, "A Day With Georgia O'Keeffe," *Art News*, December, 1977, p. 42.

5. Robert Hughes, *American Visions: The Epic History of Art in America* (New York: Knopf, 1997), p. 394.

6. O'Keeffe, pages unnumbered.

7. *Georgia O'Keeffe*, video, producer/director Perry Miller Adato, WNET/13 (Chicago: Home Vision, 1977).

Chapter 7. New Mexico

1. Anita Pollitzer, *A Woman on Paper: Georgia O'Keeffe* (New York: Simon & Schuster, 1988), p. 220.

2. Bram Dijkstra, *Georgia O'Keeffe and the Eros of Place* (Princeton, N.J.: Princeton University Press, 1998), p. 231.

3. Laurie Lisle, *Portrait of an Artist: A Biography of Georgia O'Keeffe* (New York: Washington Square Press, 1986), p. 213.

4. Roxana Robinson, *Georgia O'Keeffe: A Life* (New York: Harper & Row, 1989), p. 327.

5. Ibid., p. 336.

6. Ibid., p. 328.

7. Pollitzer, p. 220.

Chapter 8. Desert Bones

1. Jack Cowart, Juan Hamilton, and Sarah Greenough, *Georgia O'Keeffe: Art and Letters* (Boston: New York Graphic Society/Little, Brown, 1987), p. 240.

2. Dorothy Seiberling, "A Flowering in the Stieglitz Years," *Life*, March 1, 1968, p. 53.

3. Anita Pollitzer, *A Woman on Paper: Georgia O'Keeffe* (New York: Simon & Schuster, 1988), p. 229.

4. Roxana Robinson, *Georgia O'Keeffe: A Life* (New York: Harper & Row, 1989), p. 359.

5. *Georgia O'Keeffe*, video, producer/director Perry Miller Adato, WNET/13 (Chicago: Home Vision, 1977).

6. Laurie Lisle, *Portrait of an Artist: A Biography of Georgia O'Keeffe* (New York: Washington Square Press, 1986), p. 261.

Chapter 9. Ladder to the Sky

1. *Georgia O'Keeffe*, video, producer/director Perry Miller Adato, WNET/13 (Chicago: Home Vision, 1977).

2. Anita Pollitzer, *A Woman on Paper: Georgia O'Keeffe* (New York: Simon & Schuster, 1988), p. 226.

3. Georgia O'Keeffe, *Georgia O'Keeffe* (New York: Viking, 1976), pages unnumbered.

4. Laurie Lisle, *Portrait of an Artist: A Biography of Georgia O'Keeffe* (New York: Washington Square Press, 1986), p. 277.

5. Mary Lynn Kotz, "A Day with Georgia O'Keeffe," *Art News*, December 1977, p. 38.

6. Pollitzer, p. 273.

7. Leo Janos, "Georgia O'Keeffe at Eighty-Four," *Atlantic Monthly*, December, 1971, p. 116.

8. Jack Cowart, Juan Hamilton, and Sarah Greenough, *Georgia O'Keeffe: Art and Letters* (Boston: New York Graphic Society/Little, Brown, 1987), p. 10.

9. Lisle, p. 300.

10. "Georgia O'Keeffe Turns Dead Bones to Live Art," *Life*, February 14, 1938, p. 28.

11. O'Keeffe, p. 53.

12. Lisle, p. 319.

Chapter 10. A Change of Life

1. Roxana Robinson, *Georgia O'Keeffe: A Life* (New York: Harper & Row, 1989), p. 348.

2. Anita Pollitzer, *A Woman on Paper: Georgia O'Keeffe* (New York: Simon & Schuster, 1988), p. 270.

3. N. Heller and J. Williams, "Georgia O'Keeffe: The American Southwest," *American Artist,* January 1976, p. 107.

4. *Georgia O'Keeffe,* video, producer/director Perry Miller Adato, WNET/13 (Chicago: Home Vision, 1977), 60 min.

5. Robinson, p. 493.

Chapter 11. Ageless Beauty

1. Dorothy Seiberling, "A Flowering in the Steiglitz Years," *Life,* March 1, 1968, p. 53.

2. Roxana Robinson, *Georgia O'Keeffe: A Life* (New York: Harper & Row, 1989), p. 490.

3. Calvin Tomkins, "Georgia O'Keeffe—The Rose in the Eye Looked Pretty Fine," *The New Yorker,* March 4, 1974, p. 64.

4. Jack Cowart, Juan Hamilton, and Sarah Greenough, *Georgia O'Keeffe: Art and Letters* (Boston: New York Graphic Society/Little, Brown, 1987), p. 10.

5. Mitchell A. Wilder, ed., *Georgia O'Keeffe: An Exhibition of the Work of the Artist from 1915 to 1966* (Fort Worth, Texas: Amon Carter Museum of Western Art, 1966), p. 22.

6. Laurie Lisle, *Portrait of an Artist: A Biography of Georgia O'Keeffe* (New York: Washington Square Press, 1986), p. 379.

7. *Georgia O'Keeffe,* video, producer/director Perry Miller Adato, WNET/13 (Chicago: Home Vision, 1977).

8. Georgia O'Keeffe, *Georgia O'Keeffe* (New York: Viking, 1976), pages unnumbered.

9. *Georgia O'Keeffe,* video.

10. Mary Lynn Kotz, "A Day with Georgia O'Keeffe," *Art News,* December 1977, p. 40.

11. *Georgia O'Keeffe,* video.

12. Leo Janos, "Georgia O'Keeffe at Eighty-Four," *Atlantic Monthly,* December 1971, p. 117.

13. Cowart, p. 11.

14. Katherine Hoffman, *An Enduring Spirit: The Art of Georgia O'Keeffe* (Metuchen, N.J.: The Scarecrow Press, 1984), p. 128.

Chapter 12. Georgia O'Keeffe's Legacy

1. Charles C. Eldredge, *Georgia O'Keeffe* (New York: Harry N. Abrams, 1991), p. 152.

2. Edith Evans Asbury, "Georgia O'Keeffe Dead at 98: Shaper of Modern Art in U.S.," *The New York Times*, March 7, 1986, p. A 1.

3. John Russell, "An Artist Inspired by New Mexico's Landscape," *The New York Times*, March 7, 1986, p. A 17.

4. Jack Cowart, Juan Hamilton and Sarah Greenough, *Georgia O'Keeffe: Art and Letters* (Boston: New York Graphic Society/Little, Brown, 1987), p. 241.

5. Anita Pollitzer, *A Woman on Paper: Georgia O'Keeffe* (New York: Simon & Schuster, 1988), p. 266.

6. Ibid.

7. Robert Hughes, *American Visions: The Epic History of Art in America* (New York: Knopf, 1997), p. 391.

8. Asbury, p. A 1.

9. <http://www.okeeffemuseum.org/visit/about_museum.html>, (May 17, 2003).

10. Email to the author from Sherry Diebolt of the Georgia O'Keeffe Museum, September 23, 2002.

11. Georgia O'Keeffe, *Georgia O'Keeffe* (New York: Viking, 1976), p. 62.

12. Calvin Tomkins, "Georgia O'Keeffe—The Rose in the Eye Looked Pretty Fine," *The New Yorker*, March 4, 1974, p. 65.

13. Mary Lynn Kotz, "A Day with Georgia O'Keeffe," *Art News*, December 1977, p. 42.

14. Britta Benke, *Georgia O'Keeffe, 1887–1986: Flowers in the Desert* (New York: Barnes & Noble, 2001), p. 90.

15. Barbara Rose, "Georgia O'Keeffe, 1887–1986," *Vogue*, May 1986, p. 292.

Further Reading

Berry, Michael. *Georgia O'Keeffe, Painter.* New York: Chelsea House Publishers, 1988.

Cowart, Jack, Juan Hamilton, and Sarah Greenough. *Georgia O'Keeffe: Art and Letters.* (Boston: New York Graphic Society/Little Brown, 1987. (Has color plates of O'Keeffe paintings.)

Eldredge, Charles C. *Georgia O'Keeffe: American and Modern.* New Haven: Yale University Press, 1993. (Has color plates of O'Keeffe paintings.)

Georgia O'Keeffe. Videocassette. Producer/director Perry Miller Adato. WNET/13. Chicago: Home Vision, 1977.

Heller, N., and J. Williams. "Georgia O'Keeffe: The American Southwest." *American Artist,* January, 1976, pp. 76–81, 107.

Kotz, Mary Lynn. "A Day with Georgia O'Keeffe." *Art News,* December 1977, pp. 36–45.

Lisle, Laurie. *Portrait of an Artist: A Biography of Georgia O'Keeffe.* New York: Washington Square Press, 1980.

Nicholson, Lois. *The Importance of Georgia O'Keeffe.* San Diego: Lucent, 1995.

O'Keeffe, Georgia. *Georgia O'Keeffe.* New York: Viking, 1976. New York: Penguin Books, 1985. (Has color plates of O'Keeffe paintings.)

Pollitzer, Anita. *A Woman on Paper: Georgia O'Keeffe.* New York: Simon & Schuster, 1988.

Shuman, R. Baird. *Georgia O'Keeffe*. Vero Beach, Fla.: Rourke, 1993.

Sills, Leslie. *Inspirations: Stories About Women Artists*. Niles, Ill.: Whitman, 1989.

Internet Addresses

<http://www.okeeffemuseum.org>
Visit the Georgia O'Keeffe Museum in Santa Fe, New Mexico, for information about the artist and pictures of her paintings.

<http://www.cnn.com/TRAVEL/DESTINATIONS/ 9707/okeeffe.santa.fe/>
Visit Georgia O'Keeffe country and learn about her life and art.

<http://artcyclopedia.com/artists/okeeffe_georgia. html>
Visit exhibits of Georgia O'Keeffe paintings in museums across the United States.

Index

Page numbers for photographs are in **boldface** type.